STUDY GUIDE

CHRISTOPHER O'BRIEN
University of Kansas

THE HUMAN VENTURE

The Great Enterprise: A World History to 1500

VOLUME I

FOURTH EDITION

ANTHONY ESLER
College of William and Mary

PRENTICE HALL, *Upper Saddle River, New Jersey 07458*

©2000 by PRENTICE-HALL, INC.
Upper Saddle River, New Jersey 07458

ISBN 0-13-014403-7

Printed in the United States of America

CONTENTS

Preface   v

Overview I   **Ancient Civilizations: The Continental Crossroads (3500-200 B.C.E.)**   **1**

Chapter 1   Humanity Before History: Stone Age People (5000-3500 B.C.E.)   4

Chapter 2   The Walls of Babylon: The Cities of Mesopotamia (3500-500 B.C.E.)   11

Chapter 3   The Pyramid Builders: The Kingdom of Egypt (3200-100 B.C.E.)   17

Chapter 4   Moses and the Prophets: The Ancient Hebrews and Their World (1500-500 B.C.E.)   23

Chapter 5   Athena and the Philosophers: The Greek City-States (1500-200 B.C.E.)   28

Overview II   **Ancient Civilizations: The Farther Reaches (2500-200 B.C.E.)**   **34**

Chapter 6   Brahman and Lord Buddha: The Rise of Indian Civilization (2500-200 B.C.E.)   36

Chapter 7   The Age of the Sages: The Rise of the Chinese Civilization (1500-200 B.C.E.)   41

Chapter 8   African Traders and Empire Builders: Nubia and Carthage (1500-150 B.C.E.)   46

Chapter 9   America's First Civilizations: The Olmecs and Chavín Culture (1500-400 B.C.E.)   51

Chapter 10   Whirlwind Has Unseated Zeus: Cultural Evolution in History   55

Overview III   **Classical Civilizations (500 B.C.E.-C.E. 500)**   **58**

Chapter 11   The Eternal City: The Roman Empire (500 B.C.E.-C.E. 500)   60

Chapter 12   The Pillars of Persepolis: Persia and The Middle East (500 B.C.E.-C.E. 650)   66

Chapter 13   Golden Age on the Ganges: The Peoples of India (200 B.C.E.-C.E. 550)   71

Chapter 14   The Grandeur of Han China: The Chinese Empire (200 B.C.E.-C.E. 200)   76

Chapter 15   The Obelisks of Axum: Africa from the Red Sea to the Sahara   81

Chapter 16   The Pyramids of Mexico and Peru: The Americas from the Mochica to the Maya (200 B.C.E.-C.E. 900)   85

Chapter 17   The Long Voyagers: Cultural Diffusion in History   89

Overview IV   **Expanding Cultural Zones (500-1500)**   **93**

Chapter 18   Cathedral Spires: The Rise of Christendom (500-1500)   95

Chapter 19   Domes and Minarets: The Rise of Islam (600-1300)   101

Chapter 20   Merchants and Missionaries of the Indies: India and Southeast Asia (600-1500)   106

Chapter 21   The First Meritocracy: China and East Asia (600-1250)   110

Chapter 22   Lords of the Eurasian Heartland: Mongol Rule from Russia to China (1200-1400)   116

Chapter 23   Kings of Inner Africa: From Ghana to Ethiopia (600-1450)   120

Chapter 24   Conquering Peoples of the Americas: From The Toltecs to Chimu (900-1400)   125

Chapter 25   The Hinge of History: From Pluralism to Globalism   129

PREFACE TO THE STUDENT

This study guide will help you to succeed in your history course and in other courses as well. It will enable you to learn more efficiently by guiding your understanding of the textbook, *The Human Venture,* 4th. Edition Volumes I & II, by Anthony Esler. What you get out of it depends on your effort. Do not consider this study guide a substitute for the text.

This study guide is set up according to a specific study format which will be explained to you in this section. Each chapter will have the following sections: **Survey, Questions/Read, Study Skills Exercises,** and **Recite/Review.** The survey section gives you a brief overview of what the author is covering in the chapter as well as objectives for the chapter. The questions/read section will aid you in reading the material more efficiently. The study skills exercises section will have suggestions and study tips that can refine and enrich your studying and learning abilities. The recite/review section will have sample questions with references to the pages of the textbook on which the answers can be found. If you answer incorrectly, go back to the correct page and reread that part. If you still do not see why you answered it incorrectly, see your professor.

Reading a textbook several times is not an efficient way to study. The most efficient way is an active interchange guide. It is called SQ3r and is an established method of study developed by Francis Robinson (*Effective Behavior.* New York: Harper and Row, 1941). Another method will be blended in called the Six R system or Cornell System (Pauk, Walter. *How to Study in College.* 4th Ed. Boston: Houghton Mifflin, 1989). Many other study methods exist but they all share the same basic characteristics: a system of active working with your text by an overview of its main points, developing questions from the main points, taking notes and then reviewing. Following any of these methods will help you organize a large amount of information by making it more meaningful and thus easier to remember. The good student has probably learned to do this so well that it is almost unconscious. If you have not followed a system like this before, it will take practice.

SQ3r stands for **Survey, Questions, Read, Recite** and **Review.** This will be our overall system. In the **Read** section, I will elaborate on the Six R system because it gives a more detailed idea of what **Read** really means. As I said earlier, your study guide is set up to follow the elements of SQ3r in each chapter. Let's look at the separate parts of SQ3r.

The S stands for **Survey.** You should look at the overall organization of the textbook title itself as well as any introductory materials the author provides. Do Not Skip prefaces and forewords because the author will explain major organizing ideas and themes that are carried out in the book. Look at the table of contents and see what areas are covered. This does not take very long but it is a way of interacting with your text. You need to make your studying as active as possible. If you are too passive, it will be harder to concentrate. You will find yourself having read several pages without the slightest idea of what you just read. Now survey the first chapter. Look at headings and subheadings (with the Esler text, the chapter headings and subheadings are listed in an outline on the first page of each chapter). If it has a general introduction or summary, read those as well. Note that your Esler text has a summary section in each chapter. The survey section of the study guide will also provide you with some introductory material. When you start this process again with another chapter, be sure to look for connections between chapters.

The Q means **Questions.** This means turn each chapter and section title into a question or series of questions. This might seem like a little thing to you but it is not insignificant. It is again a more active way of learning.

You are interacting with the material and actively searching for the answers to the questions. Historians tend to ask questions like: "What are the causes of ...? What are the likenesses and differences between ...? What are the roots of ...? Why did this happen at this time and not another? What is the importance of ...? What is the impact of ...? What is the significance of?" This study guide will give you question(s) for the main headings of each chapter and then a more detailed series for each subheading of the chapter. Remember, you should not expect complete answers until you have read the entire section. Again remember to be alert to combining material from subsequent chapters. This is particularly useful when anticipating essay questions.

Included in each questions/read section will also be a list of terms and names headed by the word "Identify." You should apply a whole series of questions automatically to this list. A suggestion I have found helpful with my student is the line from Rudyard Kipling's poem, "The Serving Men." He said: "I had six honest serving men - They taught me all I knew: Their names were Where and What and When-and Why and How and Who." Using this pattern and applying it to all the names, events and terms you see will help your studying. You may only get partial answers in each section or chapter so always be alert to blending information from section to section and making chapter to chapter connections.

The first of the 3 r's is **Read.** With your question(s) in mind, begin to read one section at a time. Look for the main idea and supporting details that will answer your question(s). Do not be content with simple yes or no or partial answers. Imagine that you need to explain this to someone else. Look at all illustrations, maps and graphs the author provides. Your author also includes a special series called "Probing the Past" and "Voices from the Past" that provides details on chapter materials. These items are there to help you establish context, not to take up space. The authors of texts spend a great deal of time deciding what to include and how to divide and title sections. My experience is that students skip this material unless they think it is on the test. This is a very shortsighted attitude. Each of the items the author includes reinforces the material in your mind. Do not ignore these things. The same is true of appendices.

While reading, do not underline or use highlighters. Wait until you finish a section and then decide what you are going to underline or highlight. If you do it as you first read, you may find yourself with a completely underlined or highlighted page when you get done. This defeats the purpose. The way suggested here is more interactive. This is not to suggest that highlighting is the only method of recording. We will cover a few more below.

Under the first "**r**", **Read**, I would like to include some elements of the Six R method. Six R stands for **Record, Reduce, Recite, Reflect, Review** and **Recapitulate.** I will concentrate on **Record, Reduce** and **Reflect.** For **Record** you can use highlighting. You can use the outline method. Your Esler text is already set up in outline form with headings and subheadings. You can fill in the rest in a reduced form. If you outline, leave space to add material from lecture, especially if it contradicts text material or updates it.

Another useful recording system is using 3x5 note cards, especially for names and terms. Put the question, name or term on one side and the answer on the other and then you have a quick system for reciting and reviewing. When you have a few extra minutes, it is easier to pull out the cards than your textbook.

There are a number of ways to **Reduce.** You should also think in terms of reorganizing when reducing. One way to do this besides the outlines and cards mentioned earlier is with a chart. The construction of a chart will help you gather information scattered throughout a chapter or chapters. Doing a chart will force you to compare, select and write down information. This will help reinforce it in your mind. It should help anticipate as well as study for essay questions. Chart ideas will be included in the Study Skills Exercises section. Another way to record as well as reduce and reorganize is to use the Cornell system. You use a sheet of paper in which the margin line is 1/3 from the left. In that space you write your questions, names, terms, etc., and in the other 2/3's space you put the answers. Leave space to add lecture material and/or reserve reading material. (Some college bookstores carry this type of paper and it is usually called review and summary paper). When you get to the recite section, having your notes this way will be an advantage because you can cover up the answer and see how well you can give the answer. Then reverse it and see if you can recognize your questions from the answer. It is very important to cover up the answer because you want to reduce the cues. This gives you the approximate situation you will be in on the test. If you look at the question and answer at the same time, you will have false confidence.

Reflection is another element of Six R. To reflect in history, just try to imagine yourself in the place of a person of the time. If you were an Egyptian merchant, what were your activities and products? Imagine yourself as some monarch's advisor defending his or her policies. Then do the same for the other side. Be alert to parallels today. What patterns of today connect to the past? If you see your own life as history, you look back to our history to make decisions, to understand how you were shaped, to know the roots of your dreams of the future. Do this with people in the past. Be careful not to just do it for those you agree with. Be alert also to putting yourself in the historian's place. Do you see other views based on the chapter materials?

The **Study Skills Exercises** section will follow **Questions/Read.** This section will emphasize **Record, Reduce, Reflect** aspects of the Six R method. Here there will be suggestions and study tips on writing identifications, constructing charts, connecting chapters and a vocabulary section. Vocabulary will be included in each chapter in this guide. I will list up to ten per chapter that will insure your understanding of the material. If you encounter others I haven't listed, be sure and look them up!

Vocabulary is an excellent way to improve your general reading and study skills. Many entrance exams at the graduate school level make heavy use of vocabulary so you have another practical reason to improve yours. History is a good subject for trying to increase your vocabulary because there is not as much specialized jargon as in many other fields. The words historians use are terms an educated person would find useful in reading and writing.

Back to the SQ3r and the second "r" which is **Recite.** You should find yourself spending more time reciting than reading. Reciting is like rehearsing for a play. You repeat the material to yourself or to another student. Some students find forming a study group is helpful. Have each student be responsible for some particular section or chapter and teach it to the rest of you. Having to teach the material requires a great deal of interaction with your subject. You'll find that you know it better. It is to your advantage to practice so that you can recite with as few cues as possible. Whatever method(s) you used to record will now be extremely important in having an efficient system. If a test is fill in, short answer or essay, total recall is required. Multiple choice, true/false and matching questions are called recognition questions because you only have to recognize the right answer when you see it. Make sure, however, that you work at understanding the material when you read it since the professor may word it differently or ask you to choose the most correct answer, not just repeat the book. Your study guide has a recite/review section. Make sure you understand the answer. Do not just memorize the question for the same reasons as stated above.

The third "r" of SQ3r is **Review.** If you have done the things explained above, review should be just a refresher practice before the test. Psychologists find we have a savings score each time we recite and review. It takes less time each time, a plus at midterm and final exam time.

As I stated earlier, this study guide is set up to follow SQ3r. There will be study tips in the Study Skills Exercises section. For practical purposes, more of them will be in early chapters so you can immediately use them when studying for the first exam.

Hopefully you are convinced by now that just reading a textbook is not the same as studying. Reading is only one component, the object of which is to thoroughly understand the material. Studying enables you to remember and recall it well. There are many more study techniques than could be listed here, especially memory tricks. You may need time management help. If you want to improve your skills, purchasing Pauk's book may help. Another is Hardin, Jackson C.A. *College Yearbook: Making it Through the First Year.* (Ginn Press). The Association of American Publishers has some basic pamphlets on getting the most out of your education. These are free - write to the Association at One Park Avenue, New York, NY, 10016.

If you feel you need help from someone, remember most campuses have departments to help you. Check with your professor, graduate assistant or counselor. Most schools have tutoring, study skills centers or similar services for you. Use them. Do not let false pride stand in your way.

Good Luck To You.

In summary, here is the standard outline for all Study Guide chapters:

> **SURVEY**
> > **Chapter Overview**
> > **Chapter Objectives**
>
> **QUESTIONS/READ**
> > **Main Headings of the Textbook**
> > **Subheadings of the Textbook**
>
> **STUDY SKILLS EXERCISES**
> The following will be included in each chapter, but there may be additional exercises in the earlier chapters under the description: **Study Tips.**
> > **Making Connections**
> > **Reflectors**
> > **Vocabulary**
> > **Timelines**
> > **Maps**
>
> **RECITE/REVIEW**
> > **Multiple Choice**
> > **Short Answers**
> > **Extended Essay**
> > **Timeline and Map Questions**
> > **Answers**

NOTE TO INSTRUCTOR: When I chose the original Esler textbook for my global history survey course, one of the reasons I liked it was the thematic approach that it followed. The charts and questions I have in this study guide are intended to encourage this thematic approach while still having general knowledge to give it context. A good article to read on this approach is:

Sjoquist, Douglas and Steck, Douglas. "A Guide to Developing World Civilizations Courses Along Thematic and Interdisciplinary Lines," *Humanities Education*. Winter, 1991. pp. 33-42.

I have been teaching history at the community college level for twenty-seven years and have found that explaining the SQ3r study method to students is important to their success. One of my colleagues, Terri Bruce, helped me set up this type of system in class and adapt it into a review guide format. She has been teaching study skills for over twenty-five years. I think you will find this a useful guide. In constructing it, I also tried to correlate it with the Instructor's Guide that Dr. Esler wrote for his text. There are no map blanks in this guide because he feels the students learn more by drawing or tracing their own. The same thing is true with timelines. So I have tried to guide them on how to do this without doing it for them. I have also tried to guide the student to the information that Dr. Esler stresses in his suggestions. In some cases that may mean I have left out some detail in the review guide that you might feel is important. However too often student guides and Instructor's Test Guides are not connected. I have tried to avoid this because I think it is a major drawback to course planning and specifically to test construction. If the student follows the study guide as recommended, they should be able to do well on tests in which the questions are chosen from the Instructor's Guide. From a reinforcement point of view, it also helps to have a certain percentage of questions directly from the student's study guide. I have found that using about 25% directly without change encourages them to use the guide. Any less and they ignore it and too much more than that encourages them only to memorize the sample questions and ignore the more comprehensive study method.

A NOTE TO PREFACES AND INTRODUCTION

PREFACE: remember the study guide suggestions. Do not skip the preface because you learn the outlook of the author and the themes of the book. Read the Preface to the First Edition first (pp. xiii-xiv).
1. What are the aims of this text?
2. Define or explain the following terms:
   a. Global perspective
   b. Breadth of coverage
   c. Humanizing of history
   d. Strong narrative line

PREFACES TO THE SECOND AND THIRD EDITION (p. xi)
1. What elements has the author added to the book material since the first edition?
2. What roles do "in-between ages" often play in human history?

INTRODUCTION: The author continues here to tell you his concepts about the title and subject of the text. (pp. 2-3)
1. Why does your author use the word "venture?"
2. What is the human commitment to history and civilization?
3. What are the criticisms of civilization as well as responses to that criticism?
4. What is one of the major themes of the text?
5. How does the mainstream appear to those who did not choose civilization?

OVERVIEW I

ANCIENT CIVILIZATIONS: THE CONTINENTAL CROSSROADS (3500-200 B.C.E.)

This overview sets the stage for Chapters 1 to 5 and gives an important picture of what you are studying. Instead of following the format I do for the individual chapters, I will just ask a series of questions. This overview should be reviewed regularly as you read the chapters.

Questions:
1. What were the stages of social evolution from hunter-gatherers to urban dwellers?
2. What are the four great civilizations that will be discussed in this section? When did each come into being?
3. What is the significance of the eastern Mediterranean?

Map: Ancient Civilizations: The Continental Crossroads, 3500-200 B.C.E. (p. 7)

COMPARISON CHART FOR OVERVIEW I:
ANCIENT CIVILIZATIONS: THE CONTINETAL CROSSROADS.
Photocopy this chart so you can use it for Chapters 1-5 (you need at least 5 copies)

THEMES AND PATTERNS OF CIVILIZATIONS	CIVILIZATION_____ (fill in name)
Geographic and/or historic setting (include major cities)	
Government(s) (include major leaders)	
Society (include class issue, roles of women)	
Economy (growth of trade-include major cities, goods and extent of trade)	
Science and Technology	
Literacy, writing, literature	
Arts	
Ideas and Values (include religion, philosophy, political ideals)	

DIRECTIONS FOR THE TIMELINES AND CHRONOLOGIES:

It is important to keep an idea of how various events relate to each other in history to understand cause and effect. In each chapter you will find events that you should put on a timeline. This is not for the purpose of memorizing dates for a test, although if your professor says there are date questions, it is good practice. The main purpose is to see relationships. Students particularly like the comparison charts because they want a sense of knowing what is happening in each civilization at the same time. A number of them feel it is less confusing this way. I have included a series of lines that you can use to make your own timelines. Develop the sets or divisions most useful to you.

One tip-I find that many of my students get confused about centuries and millenniums. In this text the author uses the dating system B.C.E (Before the Common Era) and C.E. (Common Era). These dates correspond to the older B.C. (Before Christ) and A.D. (Anno Domini, in the year of the Lord), but without the Christian reference. In this system there is no zero year. You start with 1 B.C.E. and C.E. 1. Therefore 1 B.C.E. to 100 B.C.E is the first century B.C.E. The second century B.C.E. is 101-200 and so on. The first century C.E. 1 to 100. The second century C.E. is C.E. 101-200 and so on. The first millennium B.C.E. is from 1 B.C.E. to 1000 B.C.E. The first millennuim C.E. is from C.E. 1 to C.E. 1000. When you see ca., it means an approximate date.

TIMELINE lines: Photocopy this page as you will need at least one timeline for most of the chapters.

I have filled in the first Timeline as an example.

CHAPTER TITLE <u>Humanity before History: Stone Age People (5000-3500 B.C.E.)</u>

|_____|_____|_____|_____|_____|_____|_____|_____|_____|_____|_____|_____|_

ca. 5,000,000-10,000 B.C.E. Paleolithic period
ca. 2,000,000 B.C.E. tool production begins
ca. 500, 000 B.C.E. Ice Age, global migrations
ca. 100,000 B.C.E. religion practiced
ca. 30,000 B.C.E. Cave paintings
ca. 10,000-3500 B.C.E. Neolithic period, agriculture and villages
ca. 3500 B.C.E. History and civilizations begin

CHAPTER TITLE_____

|_____|_____|_____|_____|_____|_____|_____|_____|_____|_____|_____|_____|_

CHAPTER TITLE_____

|_____|_____|_____|_____|_____|_____|_____|_____|_____|_____|_____|_____|_

CHAPTER TITLE_____

|_____|_____|_____|_____|_____|_____|_____|_____|_____|_____|_____|_____|_

CHAPTER TITLE_____

|_____|_____|_____|_____|_____|_____|_____|_____|_____|_____|_____|_____|_

1

HUMANITY BEFORE HISTORY: STONE AGE PEOPLE (5000-3500 B.C.E.)

This study guide is based on a particular system. If you skipped the introductory material on pp. 2-6, please read it before you proceed to get the most out of your text.

SURVEY

Chapter Overview: This chapter covers the biological, cultural and social development of humans as they made the transition to civilization. Skim through the topical outline for Chapter 1 on p. 8 and then read the summary on p. 24.

Chapter Objectives: After reading the chapter and following the study methods recommended, you should be able to:

1. Summarize the development of humans biologically covering the crucial steps of evolution, migration and racial diversity.
2. Discuss the development of culture and technology in Paleolithic food gathering groups.
3. Describe and explain the significance of the technology and cultural developments of the Neolithic Age.
4. Compare the Paleolithic and Neolithic Ages in terms of technology and cultural developments.
5. Trace the development of tools and technologies at each age of human cultural evolution.
6. Trace the process of transition from simpler political, economic and social structures to the more complex ones of civilization.

QUESTIONS/READ

HUMAN DEVELOPMENT: What was the overall process of early human development? (Remember you have to read the entire section before you can answer this question completely).

Beginnings: What are the various ancient and modern ways to explain the beginnings of human life on earth? (Again remember that you have to read the whole subsection before you can answer this first question completely). What is the recognizable geography that is the stage of our adventure? Identify: seven continents, Eurasia, two largest continents, Central America.

The Bone Hunters: Who are the "bone hunters" and what discoveries have they made? What other experts have helped in understanding remains of earlier people? What are some of the controversies? Identify: Neanderthal, Olduvai George, "Lucy," Cro-Magnon, Peking Man, Java Man, "Ice Man," "African Eve."

Biological Evolution: What general biological changes took place from the first prosimian to the most developed hominid? What advantages did human progenitors have for survival: What biological development gave the capacity to go beyond biology to culture? Identify: prosimian, primates, hominid, Neanderthal, Cro-Magnon, Homo sapiens .

The Prehistoric Migrations: When, where and why did humans undertake migrations? What caused the ice age and what effects did it have: How long did it take hominids to migrate from East Africa to North China? Identify: Bering Strait.

The Human Races: How and why did racial differences develop? What three other points does the author make about racial diversity? Identify: three major racial groups, three racial remnants, Homo sapiens sapiens, races.

PALEOLITHIC FOOD GATHERERS: What types of cultural developments do we find in Paleolithic food gatherer groups?

The Food-Gathering Band: Why did food-gathering bands probably develop? What technology made this social evolution possible? What was the likely structure of social relations? Identify: Paleolithic Period, band.

Stone Age Women: What were the various roles of Stone Age women? What is the significance of "Venus figures?" Based on studying modern food-gathering cultures, what was probably true about women's freedom and influence?

Beginnings of Religion and Art: What can be reconstructed about the beginnings of religion and art from evidence left by Paleolithic groups? Identify: Shanidar, Lascaux, Les Eyzies caves at Motopo.

NEOLITHIC FARMERS: What types of cultural evolution were achieved by the Neolithic farmers?

The Discovery of Agriculture: Why was the discovery of agriculture so significant? Where did the discovery occur? Who were the discoverers? What explanations have been offered for this basic shift? Identify: Neolithic, New Stone Age, Agricultural Revolution.

Crops and Flocks: How did crops and flocks develop? How did settled agricultural grow in complexity? What were the advantages and disadvantages of this change? How did support of population per square kilometer compare? Identify: pastoralists.

Life in the Neolithic Village: What was life like in a Neolithic village? What types of handicraft technology developed? Why was the village a revolution? Identify: Skara Brae.

Alternate Lifestyles: What variety of lifestyles were there from five thousand years ago to now? How did climate and geography tend to determine distribution of these basic styles of life? What were the common crops and where was each located geographically?

THE TRANSITION TO CIVILIZATION: What was the process of transition from simpler life styles to the structures of civilization?

The First Civilizations: Where did civilization first emerge? What are the various explanations for this? Identify: "hydraulic empires," "conquest empires," civilization.

Monarchy, Hierarchy, Patriarchy: What was the essence of each of these three organizational principles that dominated most early civilizations? Identify: "private sphere," "public sphere."

Economics, Technology, Culture: What were the economic foundations of city-based civilizations? What types of technology and culture existed?

SUMMARY: What are the major points in this chapter?

STUDY SKILLS EXERCISES

1. **Study Tip:** In the preface of this guide, the skill of identification was mentioned as a useful way to study history. Use the pattern of who or what, when, where, why in identifying major terms. You can put these terms on 3x5 cards or use the Cornell method. **Be sure to incorporate any pertinent material from illustrations or maps.** It may also be useful to blend in information from various parts of the chapter or chapters. Do not expect all the relevant material to be relevant in one place. Here is an example with the term Lascaux. Note that I left out the "how," but if your professor has numerous or exclusively essay questions on test, I would include it.

Lascaux:
Who or What: a cave, Cro-Magnon people
Where: France
When: Approximate 30,000 B.C.E. , Old Stone Age or Paleolithic Era
Why: (in terms of significance-why did the author feel this was important to mention): has significant examples of beginnings of art on its walls such as bison and horses showing a high degree of artistic skill-**Do not neglect illustrations** when doing this. Your text has an example of this art on p. 17. Remember the more cues you have, the more likely that you will remember material.

2. **Making Connections:** In the preface, I mentioned reducing and rearranging information. One way to do this is to make a chart which helps you compare information in the chapter or chapters. There are two major advantages to doing this. First, you have larger elements of the chapter in a compact form to which you can add relevant lecture information. The second advantage is that doing the chart reinforces the material either for objective or essay exams. In this case, compare the Paleolithic Era to the Neolithic Era in the major categories. I have constructed the chart for you so you can see what I mean (see chart with Overview I) and then continue it on your own. In the future chapters I will alert you to similar items connecting information either within the individual chapter or between chapters. Charts are included for your own use on the last page of most chapters of the Study Guide.

3. **Reflection:** This is one of the Six R's in the study method described in the preface. Again this will reinforce as well as enrich your understanding of the material.
   a. If you were hunter-gatherer, how might you react if someone were trying to persuade you to settle down and be a farmer?
   b. Your text author mentions that earlier peoples were "masters of the earth" until they had to compete with civilization. Consider what situation we would be in if we suddenly lost all our modern conveniences and had to survive as hunter-gatherers. What would our priorities be? What would we need to survive? Would surviving hunter-gatherers be masters again?
   c. Some people today who like the "survivalist" mode see it as a type of "rugged individualism" yet your author points out that survival was always a "cooperative venture." Consider the development of social organization from Paleolithic to early civilized societies.
   d. Your author has excellent thought and reflection questions in many of the illustration captions. The boxes with "Probing the Past" and "Voices from the Past" also have good questions. Make it a habit to make use of them. Too many students skip illustrations. They give you context cues to remembering material. I will not continuously list these in each **reflection** section. Make sure you remember to do this for each chapter.

4. **Timeline:** Putting things in chronological order helps you relate and compare them to each other. This is something you should do even of your instructor says there are no dates on the test. Again it gives you cues and context to remember things. Put the following events on the line below:
   a. Know the system of five that your author mentions on page 10.
   b. Draw the line below on a separate piece of paper and put the following items in relative time positions to each other.
      from 5 to 3 1/2 million years ago Appearance of hominids

      500,000 years ago Ice Age Migrations
      200,000 years ago African Eve
      125,000 years ago Neanderthal
      100,000 years ago Seeds of Religion
      70 to 40,000 years ago Migration to Australia
      40 to 20,000 years ago Migration to Americas
      35,000 years ago Cro-Magnon
      5 million to 10,000 B.C.E. Paleolithic Era/Old Stone Age
      8000 B.C.E. Beginnings of Agriculture
      10,000 to 3500 B.C.E. Neolithic Age/New Stone Age
      3500 B.C.E. Beginnings of Civilization
      500 years ago or around 1500 C.E. Modern History

5 million years   3500 B.C.E.   Present

5. **Maps:** Again maps are useful for giving cues and context in learning and remembering information. As with dates, do these exercises even if you do not have them on a test.

    a. Trace a map of the world from the textbook and then enlarge it on a photocopier. You could probably buy an outline map in your bookstore but tracing it will help you remember it better. Put the following locations from chapter one on it. You should consult an Atlas. If you are "rusty" about geography, I would put in oceans, major mountain ranges, rivers and deserts. This book assumes you are geographically literate.

        Asia Iraq   Mesopotamia
        Europe France Egypt
        Africa Zimbabwe   Japan
        Australia Russia Nile River
        North America Jericho Tigris and Euphrates River
        South America India Indus River
        Central America Kalahari Desert Huanghe (Yellow) River
        Bering Strait

    b. **Global Distribution of Hominids and Homo Sapiens:** (p. 14) Using general geographical area in your description, write a paragraph that compares the global distribution of early hominids to Homo Erectus to Homo Sapiens.

    c. **Recession of Hunter-Gatherers:** (p. 19) Write a paragraph based on this map that describes the receding of hunter-gatherers from 8000 B.C.E. to the present. Where are most surviving hunter-gatherers today? Why do you think they are in these particular areas?

    d. **Expansion of Agriculturalists:** (p. 21) Compare the three maps and then write a paragraph describing the expansion of agriculturalists. What areas have the least expansion of agriculture? Look at an atlas and find out what types of area these are.

RECITE/REVIEW

This section has a sampling of multiple choice, short essay and extended questions that you should be able to answer when you have completed the chapter and followed the study techniques recommended. After the essay sections, you will find a separate section with questions on timelines, maps and geographical material from the text. The answers are listed at the end. Some of the questions require analysis, not just memory. If you missed a question, return to the chapter and study that section again.

Multiple Choice

1. Which one of the following would we LEAST notice as anything but a modern person walking through the New York subway?
    a. Prosimian
    b. primates
    c. Lucy
    d. Cro-Magnon

2. If they had only moved at an average of ten miles per generation, how many years would it have taken early hominids to go from East Africa to North China?
    a. 5000
    b. 15,000
    c. 25,000
    d. 50,000

3. The three major racial groups are
    a. Prosimian, primate and hominid.
    b. Neanderthal, Cro-Magnon and Homo sapiens.
    c caucasoid, mongoloid and negroid.
    d. bushmanoid, pygmoid and astroloid.

4. Based on studying modern hunter-gatherer bands, Paleolithic bands probably had no more than
    a. two or three dozen individuals.
    b. two to three hundred individuals.
    c. a thousand people.
    d. five thousand people.

5. A Paleolithic band would have been LEAST likely to have
    a. religious beliefs.
    b. fire and stone implements.
    c. domesticated sheep and cattle herds.
    d. artists.

6. Sites in Lascaux, France and the Motopo hill in Zimbabwe are celebrated examples of
    a. Venus figures
    b. prehistoric art.
    c. metal working.
    d. agricultural beginnings.

7. Both the motives and the means for the earliest human migration was provided by
    a. constant warfare between Paleolithic bands.
    b. climatic changes of the ice age.
    c. overpopulation.
    d. the Agricultural Revolution.

8. Objects showing artistic developments found in Paleolithic sites include
    a. sculpture, painting and music.
    b. ceramics, textiles and paintings
    c. architecture, metal figurines and writings.
    d. jewelry, mosaics and buildings.

9. The climax of prehistory and the foundation of civilization would be the
    a. ice age.
    b. beginning of religion.
    c. development of monarchy
    d. Agricultural Revolution.

10. Civilization emerged first in
    a. Mesopotamia, Egypt, N. India and NE China.
    b. Japan, SE Asia and Central America.
    c. Egypt, S. China and India and South America.
    d. northern and southern Asia.

11. As indicated by the term "hydraulic empire," most early civilizations began by
    a. the oceans.
    b. at strategic straits.
    c. rivers.
    d. sea and trade routes.

12. Skara Brae was significant as
    a. the first of the Near East Hydraulic Empire.
    b. a walled and moated Neolithic village.
    c. the first site of the Agricultural Revolution.
    d. a site for the earliest evidence of Paleolithic religious artifacts.

13. Which one of the following was **NOT** a new skill found in the early urban-imperial cultures?
    a. weaving cloth
    b. working in metals
    c. monumental architecture
    d. written language

Short Essay

14. Some historians and anthropologists have argued that the term "hunter-gathering" should be expressed as "gathering-hunting." Why would they argue this? Include your own view in your answer.
15. Describe the biological changes that took place in the development of hominids.
16. Describe "Venus figures" and their possible meanings.

Extended Essay

17. Discuss the general biological evolution of human ancestors including a discussion of the advantages of stereoscopic and colored vision, bipedal walking, oppositive thumb and larger brain capacity.
18. Compare the development of social organization from Paleolithic to Neolithic to early civilization.
19. Discuss the shift from the hunter-gatherer technology to pastorialism to agriculture. Evaluate the use of the term "revolution" in the phrase Agricultural Revolution.
20. Discuss the part that women played in the Paleolithic and Neolithic Eras.

Timeline and Map Questions: The questions here are from the timeline and maps but there are also other types of geographical questions included in the text.

21. Which one of the following is NOT one of the "5" system that gives you a rough chronological perspective of human evolution and history?
    a. last 500 years=modern history
    b. 5000 years ago=civilization
    c. 50,000 years ago=appearance of African Eve
    d. 5,000,000 million years ago=appearance of hominids

22. The Neolithic or New Stone Age is generally dated beginning in
    a. 50,000 B.C.E.
    b. 15,000 B.C.E.
    c. 10,000 B.C.E.
    d. 3,500 B.C.E.

23. Which one of the following is NOT correct in relation to the ice age and migration?
    a. 500,000 B.C.E. ice age begins and humans move northward
    b. Hominids reach China three to four thousand years ago
    c. 70,000 to 40,000 B.C.E. humans reach Australia
    d. By 20,000 B.C.E. humans reached Europe

24. The largest continent is
    a. Europe.
    b. Asia.
    c. Africa.
    d. North America.

25. Most of human prehistory appears to have developed on the continent of
    a. Asia
    b. Africa
    c. South America
    d. Australia

26. Water covers what proportion of the earth's surface?
   a. one-fourth
   b. one-third
   c. one-half
   d. two-thirds

27. Which area was NOT part of the earliest expansion of agriculturalists by 3000 B.C.E.?
   a. Africa
   b. Asia
   c. Europe
   d. North America

ANSWERS

Multiple Choice:
1. d, p.12
2. b, p. 13
3. c, p. 13
4. a, p. 15
5. c, pp. 15-17
6. b, p. 17
7. b, p. 12
8. a, pp. 16-17
9. d, pp. 17-18
10. a, p. 22
11. c, p. 22
12. b, p. 20
13. a, pp. 20, 23

Short Essay:
14. p. 16
15. p. 12
16. p. 16

Extended Essay:
17. pp. 10-12
18. pp. 15-23
19. pp. 15-22
20. pp. 16-20

Timeline and Maps:
21. c, p. 10
22. c, p. 18
23. d, p. 13
24. b, pp. 9-10
25. b, pp. 10, 12
26. d, p. 9
27. d, p. 21

* While there are specific page numbers on most of the essay questions, it should always be understood that your short essays and extended essays will include pertinent material from the "Probing the Past" and "Voices from the Past" as well as from the illustrations/maps and their captions. "Making Connections" essay questions may have pertinent chapters rather than specific page number because of the variety of choices you may make to answer the question.

2

THE WALLS OF BABYLON: THE CITIES OF MESOPOTAMIA (3500-500 B.C.E.)

(handwritten margin notes) ① aristocrats: ① royal officials, ② members of royal family ③ chief priests of major temples. ② middle-class: ① merchants ② traders ③ Artisans ③ lower class: ① tenant farmers ② serfs

SURVEY

Chapter Overview: This chapter covers the first known development of civilization. It took place in the land between the rivers, or Mesopotamia, modern-day Iraq. Read Overview I, look at the topical outline on p. 26 and then read the summary on pp. 38-39 before beginning this chapter.

Chapter Objectives: After reading this chapter, you should be able to:

1. Describe Mesopotamia and the development of society within it.
2. Trace the rise and fall of empires within Mesopotamia.
3. Discuss the impediments to empire as well as the methods by which empire was gained.
4. Outline the various accomplishments of Mesopotamia culture.
5. **Making Connections:** Summarize the development of religion from the first seeds in the Paleolithic Era to the Neolithic to Mesopotamia.

QUESTIONS/READ

MESOPOTAMIAN SOCIETY: What were the major aspects of Mesopotamian society? *(handwritten: Greeks? that brought to be Mesopotamian cities used Mesopotamia)*

(handwritten: Mesopotamia: present-day Iraq)

A Land Between Two Rivers: What and where was the land between two rivers? What was the direction of the center of civilization and the three areas involved? Identify: Near East, Tigris, Euphrates, tells, Sumeria, Akkadian Babylon, Assyria. *(handwritten: war-like. 1000'-600 BC. Nineveh: Assurbanipal Iraq Mesopotamia fast-moving river slow moving river shapeless mounds of broken down buildings Hammurabi of Akkad 1800 - 1600 BC)*

Irrigation, Building, Bronze Age Crafts: What type of irrigation, buildings and Bronze Age crafts marked the beginnings of the ancient Sumerians? Identify: Uruk, Lagash, Ur, Babylon, Nineveh. *(handwritten: Babylon Assyrian capital. dikes, canals, irrigation ditches)*

The City and the City State: What were the first cities and city states like physically? How were they structured socially? How did the irrigation systems function? What was the status of women in Sumer Babylon? Identify: ziggurats, shaduf. *(handwritten: walled; 4 gates(1 in each wall) town divided into quarters. temples pyramid terraced pivoted pole; weight on one end bucket on other. dams protect crops from flood canals carry runoff; shaduf applies.)*

The Palace and the Temple: What was the connection between the palace and the temple? What were the characteristics of Mesopotamian religion? What was the function of the patron-god or goddess? What was the job of the priests? What was the status of royalty in relation to civilization? How did the power of the kings grow in Sumerian times to Assyrian times? Identify: Ensi. *(handwritten: polytheistic could work, own property engage in business, etc. war-leader of city Bring rising water rich harvest maintain more powerful Came 1st in Sumeria Kings= Stewards of Gods. dress & feed statue plays music Ensi gained power in emergencies did not recie)*

MESOPOTAMIAN EMPIRE: What were the various empires that established themselves in Mesopotamia? *(handwritten: Became more & more ① flat ② land open to nomadic invasions ③ fragmented feudal order)*

Impediments to Empire: What impediments were there to empire building in the Tigris-Euphrates valley? What were the four successful attempts at empire building? Identify: Sargon, Hammurabi, feudalism, petty-satism. *(handwritten: when individual cities war w/ each other)*

(handwritten: Sumeria O. Bab. Assyria N. Bab. 1st Empire Builder builder of O. Bab.)

Sargon of Akkad: Who was Sargon of Akkad and what success did he have at empire building? How did he accomplish it? Identify: Agade.

Hammurabi of Babylon: Who was Hammurabi and what was his success at empire building? What is the symbolism of Babylon? At what two times did Babylon have supremacy? What was the Code of Hammurabi and why was it significant?

The Assyrian Warfare Status: What was the nature of the Assyrian warfare state? What was the extent of their empire? What tactics did they use to conquer and hold their lands? What or who brought an end to the empire? Identify: Assur, Assurbanipal, Nineveh.

Nebuchadnezzar and the New Babylon Empire: Who was Nebuchadnezzar and what was his success at empire building? What was the extent of the empire? What structures did he build? Who eventually conquered the empire? What does Mesopotamia claim as a "first?" Identify: Ishtar Gate, Hanging Gardens of Babylon, Cyrus the Great.

MESOPOTAMIAN CULTURE: What were the characteristics and accomplishments of Mesopotamian culture?

Polytheistic Religions: What are polytheistic religions and why did they develop as they did in Mesopotamia? What does a developed religion require? How did religion become more elaborate? What changes occurred over time in views and metaphors of gods? Identify: numinous, Anu, Enlil, Ninhursag, Utu, Sin, Ishtar, Marduk, Assur.

Writing, Learning and Literature: What advances took place in writing, learning and literature? What developments occurred in math and astronomy? What is the *Epic of Gilgamesh* and the story it tells? Identify: pictographs, cuneiform, phonographs, scribes, libraries, Gilgamesh, Enkiddu.

The Arts, Gold and Lapis Lazuli: What were the various aspects of the arts and what place did gold lapis lazuli have within? Identify: ziggurat, Lion Hunt frieze, cylinder seal, Ishtar gate.

SUMMARY: What are the main points of this chapter?

STUDY SKILLS EXERCISES

1. **Study Tip:** Don't forget to look at the chapter outline (p. 26) in this chapter and in all the chapters. Remember to make an outline work for you by adding your own details. At the very minimum, you should be able to recognize or identify every name in the main and subheadings after you read the chapter.

2. **Making Connections:** Make a chart comparing the various themes and patterns of civilization in each civilization you study. The chart is at the end of this unit and will be a constant to add to from Chapters 1 to 5. This type of chart is very useful for studying concepts and preparing for essay questions. In doing the chart, you have to analyze and synthesize to complete it. At the end of each overview section, you can put the charts side by side to look for recurring themes and patterns from one civilization to another. Most essay test questions fall in this category. If they are simply repeating in summary form what is in the text, you are still well-prepared.

3. **Reflection:**
   a. Make sure that you look at the illustrations and read the captions. Consider the questions asked there. Do the same thing with the "Voices From the Past."
   b. If you were an archaeologist and could only find physical remains of Mesopotamian cities and city states, what kinds of conclusions could you draw about the society, government and religion of the Mesopotamians?
   c. What are the risks of deducing what a society is like based on its law code?

4. **Timeline:** See Timeline Directions and blanks at the end of this chapter.

2300 B.C.E.	Sargon of Akkad
1792-1750 B.C.E.	Hammurabi
1800-1600 B.C.E.	Old Time Babylon
8-7th centuries B.C.E.	Assyrian Empire
7th century B.C.E.	Assurbinipal
605-562 B.C.E.	Nebuchanezzar II
6th century B.C.E.	New Babylonian Empire
539 B.C.E.	Babylonia falls to Persians

3000 B.C.E.	2500 B.C.E.	2000 B.C.E.	1500 B.C.E.	500 B.C.E.

(This is a **sample** of the way you might put in the dates -use the blanks at the end of this chapter)

5. **Maps:**
    a. **Ancient Civilization of Eurasia, 3500-1500 B.C.E.:** (p. 28) What were the four earliest centers of Eurasian Civilization? What area did the Assyrian migrate from?
    b. **Ancient Civilizations: The Continental Crossroads, 3500-200 B.C.E.:** (p. 7) Trace another world map and be able to locate the basic ancient civilization centers.

Mesopotamia   Shang, Zhou and Qin of China
Egypt   Kush
Indus Culture   Carthaginian Empire
Ganges Culture   Olmec Culture

RECITE/REVIEW

Multiple Choice

1. Which one of the following has the **LEAST** association with the other three?
    a. Mesopotamia
    b. Iraq
    c. Euphrates
    d. Turkey

2. Mesopotamian temples were characterized by ziggurats. These were
    a. elaborate irrigation systems.
    b. monumental gateways in the high city walls.
    c. the four quarters or zones of the city.
    d. tall pyramidal terraced towers.

3. Which one of the following was **NOT** part of a small middle class developing in the Mesopotamian city state?
    a. skilled artisans in textiles and metals
    b. merchants
    c. long distance traders
    d. chief priests

4. The position of hereditary monarch in Mesopotamia probably developed from a city governor and war leader called the
    a. Enki.
    b. Enkiddu.
    c. Ensi.
    d. Satrapy.

5. One of the forces that worked against unification of Mesopotamia was petty-statism. This was a tendency to
    a. breakup into smaller states, none with enough power to conquer the other.
    b. fight class wars between the free peasants and tenant farmers.
    c. feud between priestly class and nobles for influence over the king.
    d. polarization of great rivals.

6. The first Sumerian king to unify much of the Tigris Empire valley around 2300 B.C.E. was Sargon of
    a. Akkad
    b. Chaldea
    c. Assyria
    d. Amorite.

7. Which one of the following leaders is **NOT** correctly matched to kingdom?
    a. Sargon = Akkad
    b. Hammurabi = Old Babylonia
    c. Assurbinapal = Assyria
    d. Nebuchadnezzar II = Persia

8. Which one of the following is **NOT** part of Hammurabi's Code of Laws?
    a. It reflected an eye for an eye philosophy.
    b. The society had little social hierarchy.
    c. There was a highly developed belief in social justice.
    d. It expressed the conviction that might did not make right.

9. Among the conquerors of Mesopotamia, the ones that were most brutal and violent were the
    a. Sumerians
    b. Akkadians
    c. Assyrians.
    d. Chaldeans.

10. Babylon is to the Chaldeans as Nineveh is to the
    a. Sumerians
    b. Amorites
    c. Persians.
    d. Assyrians.

11. Babylon's hanging gardens were one of the Seven Wonders of the World under the rule of the
    a. Amorites
    b. Chaldeans (Nebuchadnezzar)
    c. Assyrians.
    d. Sumerians.

12. Sumerians scribes developed a style of writing or script called
    a. cuneiform
    b. shaduf
    c. ziggurat.
    d. lapis lazuli.

13. We owe the following to Mesopotamian mathematicians.
    a. number of feet in a mile
    b. geometry
    c. Arabic numerals
    d. sixty minute hour

14. In the ancient world, Chaldean was a synonym for
    a. warrior
    b. astronomer
    c. geographer.
    d. poet.

15. Which one of the following is **NOT** a major art form of the Mesopotamians?
     a. cylinder seals
     b. work with lapis lazuli
     c. Lions of the Ishtar Gate
     d. arches

Short Essay

16. Define the term "numinous" and explain the problem with building a religion on it.
17. What is a shaduf and why was it significant to the Mesopotamians?

Extended Essay

18. How were the chief characteristics of civilization evident in Mesopotamia?
19. Discuss the significance of a code of law such as Hammurabi's. Include a discussion of the information it gives
     us about the society as well as the inaccuracy of the name, Hammurabi's Code.

Timeline and Maps

20. Which one of the following is the correct order of the various Mesopotamian kingdoms?
     a. Sumerians, Akkadians, Old Babylonians, Assyrians and Chaldeans
     b. Old Babylonians, New Babylonians, Assyrians, and Akkadians
     c. Chaldeans, Akkadians, Sumerian, New Babylonians and Persians
     d. Amorites, Sumerians, Old Babylonians and Akkadians

21. The Amorite Babylonian Kingdom associated with the Hammurabi lasted from
     a. 2300 to 2000 B.C.E.   c. 900 to 700 B.C.E.
     b. 1800 to 1600 B.C.E.   d. 605 to 539 B.C.E.

22. Which one of the following was **NOT** one of the earliest centers of Eurasian civilization?
     a. Egypt
     b. Harappan India
     c. Shang China
     d. Italic Europe

23. The Tigris and Euphrates Rivers are significant to this civilization:
     a. Mesopotamia
     b. Minoan Crete
     c. Shang China
     d. Egypt

ANSWERS

Multiple Choice:
1. d, p. 27
2. d, p. 29
3. d, p. 29
4. c, p. 31
5. a, p. 31
6. a, p. 32
7. d, p. 35
8. b, p. 33
9. c, pp. 33-34
10. d, p. 34
11. b, p. 37

12. a, p. 37
13. d, p. 37
14. b, p. 37
15. d, pp. 37-38

Short Essay:
16. pp. 35-36
17. pp. 29-30

Extended Essay:
18. pp. 35-38
19. p. 33

Timeline and Maps:
20. a, whole chapter
21. b, p. 32
22. d, p. 28
23. a, pp. 27-28

3

THE PYRAMID BUILDERS: THE KINGDOM OF EGYPT (3200-100 B.C.E.)

SURVEY

Chapter Overview: Egypt was the second site in the development of civilization. Reread the Ancient Civilizations Overview, pp. 5-7, look at the chapter outline on p. 40 and read the summary on p. 54.

Chapter Objectives: After reading this chapter and following SQ3r, you should be able to:

1. Describe the basic characteristics of the Old, Middle and New Kingdoms.
2. Compare the three time periods above with an emphasis on the continuities of Egyptian civilization.
3. Summarize the major successes of the Egyptians intellectually and artistically.
4. Define and trace the elements of conservatism throughout the Kingdom of the Nile.
5. List and analyze the factors that combined to produce the order and stability of Egypt, especially in the Old Kingdom period.
6. **Making Connections**: Compare the advances of Mesopotamia and Egypt toward developing civilization.

QUESTIONS/READ

THE PYRAMID AGE: When was the Pyramid Age and what was its significance?

Egypt-The Gift of the Nile: Why is Egypt referred to as the "gift of the Nile?" How did the Egyptians differ from Mesopotamia in government and unity? What were the "two lands" of Egypt? Identify: Upper Egypt, Lower Egypt, Thebes, Memphis.

Egypt and Africa: What is the connection between Egypt and Africa? What are the cultural and political parallels between Egypt and Africa? Iedntify: Cheik Anta Diop, matrilineal descent.

The Pharaohs Unify the Land: How did the pharaohs unify Egypt? What were the characteristics of early agricultural villages of Egypt? What outside influences occurred? How did Egypt compare to Mesopotamia in terms of the city-state? What happened to the "two lands" by 3000 B.C.E.? What were the significant features of the Old Kingdom? Identify: Menes, Old Kingdom, Middle Kingdom, New Kingdom, Memphis.

The Old Kingdom: The Pyramid Builders: What were the significant features of the Old Kingdom? What were the resistances and challenges to unity? How did the pharaohs hold Egypt together? What is the difference between the Mesopotamian religious-political connection and that of the Egyptians? How was the will of the god-king carried out and what was the function of each office? What was the social structure of the Old Kingdom? Identify: nomes, Re, Ma'at, vizier, nomarchs, fellahin, great pyramid at Giza.

The Middle Kingdom: A Bridge Between Two Worlds: When was the Middle Kingdom and how did it form a bridge between two worlds? What brought an end to the Old Kingdom? How was the Middle Kingdom different from the Old? What was the Hyksos invasion and what changes did they bring? Identify: First Intermediate Period, Hyksos, Second Intermediate Period.

THE EGYPTIAN EMPIRE: When was the Egyptian Empire? How was it gained and what area did it encompass?

The New Kingdom: The Turn Toward Empire: When was the New Kingdom and why did it turn toward empire? How was it achieved? Identify: Ahmose I, Amon.

Queen Hatshepsut and Thutmose the Conqueror: What were the contributions of these two leaders to the Egyptian Empire? How did Hatshepsut achieve power and what made her unique? What was the extent of commercial development under Hatshepsut and the New Kingdom? Who replaced her and what did he add to the empire? Identify: "Byblos travelers," Fertile Cresent.

Akhenaton, the Heretic Pharaoh: Why is Akhenaton regarded as a heretic? What were the basic ideas of his new religion? How successful was he in promoting it? Identify: Nefertiti, Aton, Amenhotep, IV, Akhetaton, El-Amarna.

Final Glories and a Long Decline: What were the final glories of the empire and why did it decline? What different peoples invaded Egypt?

Rich and Poor, Men and Women: How was Egyptian society structured? What was the image and reality of the fellahin? What was the condition of women? Identify: matrilineal society.

THE WISDOM OF THE EGYPTIANS: What achievements make up the wisdom of the Egyptians? How does it compare to the Mesopotamians?

Hieroglyphics, Science, and Literature: What was hieroglyphic writing? What advances did Egyptians make in science and literature? What were the major types of Egyptian literature? Identify: hieratic, "wisdom literature," *Story of Sinuhe.*

Pyramids, Obelisks, and the Egyptian Canon: How did the pyramids, obelisks and "canon" illustrate Egyptian wisdom? What were the artistic and architectural achievements of the Old and New Kingdoms? Identify: pyramid of Khufu, Aswan, Karnak, Abu Simbel, Armana period.

Many Gods and Eternal Life: What were the views of the Egyptians on gods and eternal life? What was the most popular Egyptian myth? What was the Egyptian view of death and immortality? What was the Egyptian first relation to immortality? Identify: Re, Amon, Isis, Osiris, ankh, *Book of the Death*, Ma'at.

SUMMARY: What were the main points of the chapter?

STUDY SKILLS EXERCISES

1. **Study Tip:** Make the timelines or chronologies you do in each chapter work for you by asking yourself the following questions as you construct it. The value of doing this is as a type of review and reinforcer for the material. What time span is being covered? What is the significance of this particular time span? What are the major events covered in this chapter? How do they connect to the chapter title? Who are the significant people as groups or as individuals involved in these events? What are the significant places? What important terms and concepts are connected to these events?

2. **Making Connections**:
   a. Mesopotamia and Egypt were the first civilizations. You can compare them on many levels. The easiest way to do this is with a chart which I have provided at the end of Overview I. You should do a chart for each civilization you study. It is much easier to compare each civilization within the same category such as government, economy and so on. Your professor is likely to ask these kinds of questions in an essay test. Preparing these charts consistently from Chapters 1 to 5 will give you a good overview.
   b. Another question to consider is unity. What factors accounted for Egyptian success at unity compared to the Mesopotamian experience?
   c. What might a typical Egyptian have said to Gilgamesh about his search for eternal life?

3. **Reflections:**
    a. Be aware of the large time span covered in these chapters. From the Old Kingdom to the New covers 3000 years. An Egyptian of the New Kingdom viewing the great pyramid of Giza was looking at something built hundreds of years earlier. What effect might this have had on the New Kingdom viewer?
    b. Your author reflects to the conservatism of Egyptians throughout the chapter. What would be the advantages and disadvantages of this to Egyptians?
    c. Note all illustrations and the Voices from the Past and consider the questions and comments of the author.

4. **Timeline:** Place the following on the timeline below:
    3200 B.C.E.   Beginning of Egyptian Civilization
    3000   Unifying of Upper and Lower Egypt under Menes
    2700-2200   Old Kingdom
    2050-1800   Middle Kingdom
    1700   Invasion of Hyksos
    1550   Ahmose I drives Hyksos out
    1500-1100   New Kingdom
    1000 to 30 B.C.E.   Decline and Foreign Rulers

5. **Maps:**
    a. **Ancient Civilizations: The Continental Crossroads, 3500-200 B.C.E.** (p. 7) Be able to describe the location of the Egyptians relative to their groups.
    b. **Ancient Civilizations of Eurasia 3500-1500 B.C.E.** (p. 28) Describe and locate the sources of the Nile. What areas did the Egyptian Kingdom cover at its height? What direction did the Hyksos come from? Look at the list of foreign invaders of Egypt in your chapter and then locate as many of them as you can on this map.
    c. **Ancient Egypt** (p.42) Locate the major sites in this chapter: Nile River, Upper Egypt, Lower Egypt, Nubia, Thebes, Karnak, Akhetaton (El-Amarna), Memphis, Fertile Cresent.

RECITE/REVIEW

Multiple Choice

1. The major Egyptian political unit throughout its history was the
    a. polis.   c. centralized monarchical state.
    b. village.   d. city-state.

2. The traditional "two lands" of Egypt refers to
    a. Upper Egypt in the south and Lower Egypt in the north.
    b. Nubia and the South.
    c. Old and New Kingdoms.
    d. Area of foreigners and area of native Egyptians.

3. Historian Cheik Anta Diop has emphasized that Egyptian culture was influenced by
    a. Mesopotamia.   c. Greece.
    b. Africa.   d. the Hebrews.

4. Which one of the following is NOT correctly matched?
    a. Old Kingdom-pyramid builders
    b. First Intermediate Period-political disruption and famine
    c. Middle Kingdom-longest lasting of the Egyptian kingdoms
    d. New Kingdom-period of empire

5. If you were a monarch in ancient Egypt, you would be
    a. a priest in the temple of the pharaoh.
    b. a peasant working on royal or noble lands.
    c. the chief administrative officer and general right hand to the pharaohs.
    d. governor and military leader of a major providence.

6. A ruling principle of the pharaoh and administrative officials was Ma'at. This meant
    a. that the pharaoh was god-king.
    b. the principle of unity that helped Upper and Lower Egypt together.
    c. virtues of truth, justice and order.
    d. honoring the Aton, the sun disk itself.

7. Which pharaoh is not correctly matched to a major accomplishment or program?
    a. Menes-unifying Egypt in 3000 B.C.E.
    b. Hatshepsut-queen who expanded New Kingdom trade
    c. Thutmose III-expanded the Egyptian empire
    d. Amenhotep IV-defeated and drove out the Hyksos

8. The invasion of Hyksos in the Second Intermediate period brought an end to the Middle Kingdom. Which one of the following best describes this event?
    a. The Hyksos burst out of Nubia and rapidly conquered Egypt and the Fertile Cresent.
    b. The Hyksos slowly migrated into Egypt and gradually took over ruling.
    c. A highly advanced people, the Hyksos brought new religion and art.
    d. The Hyksos contributed very little to Egyptian culture or technology.

9. Which one of the following is not a god or goddess of the Egyptians?
    a. Isis   c. Ankh
    b. Osiris   d. Amon

10. Cuneiform was to the Mesopotamians as _____ was to Egyptians.
    a. hieroglyphic   c. fellahin
    b. hieratic   d. sinuhe

11. This particular art form broke away from the rigid "canon" of Egyptian arts:
    a. Karnak   c. Abu Simbal
    b. Amarna   d. Aswan

12. The Egyptian *Book of the Dead* was a
    a. collection of wisdom literature and poetry.
    b. tale of a noble Egyptian who is exiled from his native land.
    c. list of deceased pharaohs and their great exploits for Egypt.
    d. collection of spells and responses to guide the soul.

Short Essay

13. What are Hieroglyphics, and how were they used?
14. What is the significance of Amenhotep IV changing his name to Akhenaton?
15. What did the cities of Thebes, Memphis and Akhetaton have in common in Egyptian history?

Extended Essay

16. Discuss the glories of Egypt as symbolized by cities of Giza, Aswan, Karnak, El-Amarna and Abu Simbel.
17. Compare the Old, Middle and New Kingdoms in terms of their legacy to Egyptian greatness.
18. Describe everyday life for Egyptian men and women at various levels of society.
19. (Making Connections) Why was early Egypt able to achieve more unity than Mesopotamia? Discuss and analyze all the factors that might have been involved.

Timeline and Maps

20. Which one of the following is the proper order of events?
    a. Old Kingdom, Invasion of Hyksos, New Kingdom, Decline and Foreign Rule
    b. Invasion of Hyksos, Old Kingdom, New Kingdom, Decline and Foreign Rule
    c. Invasion of Hyksos, Decline and Foreign Rule, Old Kingdom, New Kingdom
    d. Old Kingdom, New Kingdom, Invasion of Hyksos, Foreign Rule

21. Which one of the following has the pharaohs in correct order?
    a. Akhentaton, Menes, Thumose III, Hatshepsut, Ahmose I
    b. Menes, Ahmose I, Akhentaton, Thumose III, Hatshepsut
    c. Menes, Hatshepsut, Ahmose I, Akhenaton, Thumose III
    d. Menes, Ahmose I, Hatshepsut, Thumose III, Akhentaton

22. When invading Egypt, the Hyksos came from the
    a. Mediterranean Sea.   c. upper part of old Egypt.
    b. Near East.   d. Sahara Desert.

23. Thebes was to Upper Egypt as_____was to Lower Egypt.
    a. Memphis   c. Abu Simbel
    b. Karnak   d. Giza

24. The capital of Akhenaton built by the pharaoh Amenhotep was originally the village of
    a. Giza.   c. Nubia.
    b. Aswan.   d. El Amarna.

ANSWERS

Multiple Choice:
1. c, p. 43
2. a, p. 41
3. b, p. 41
4. c, p. 45
5. d, p. 44
6. c, p. 43
7. d, pp. 45-46
8. b, p. 45
9. c, p. 52
10. a, p. 51
11. b, p. 52
12. d, p. 53

Short Essay:
13. p. 51
14. p. 48
15. pp.,45-46, 48

Extended Essay:
16. pp. 44, 51-52
17. pp. 43-49
18. pp. 49-51
19. Chapters 2 and 3

Timeline and Maps:
20. a, pp. 43-49
21. d, pp. 43-48
22. b, p. 45
23. a, p. 41
24. d, p. 48

4

MOSES AND THE PROPHETS: THE ANCIENT HEBREWS AND THEIR WORLD (1500-500 B.C.E.)

SURVEY

Chapter Overview: In the Near East, the Hebrews and Persians make contributions to the Ancient civilizations between 1000 and 500 B.C.E. See chapter outline on page 56 and read the summary on p. 64.

Chapter Objectives: After reading this chapter, you should be able to:

1. List the various satellite civilizations in the Near East and their contributions to civilization.
2. Discuss the societies and major contributions of the Hittites and the Phoenicians
3. Trace the evolution of Hebrew religion beginning with Abraham.
4. Discuss the geographic features of the Middle East and their effects on the history of the area.
5. Discuss the rise and fall of the Hebrew kingdom.
6. **Making Connections:** Compare Hebrew society with that of the Babylonians.

QUESTIONS/READ

TURBULENT CENTURIES: When were the turbulent centuries and why are they called that?

The Near East in Tumult: Why was the Near East in tumult? What was achieved in spite of confusion and chaos? Identify: satellite cultures.

The Hittites and the Iron Age: Who were the Hittites and what connection do they have to the Iron Age? Where was the Hittite Kingdom located? Identify: Indo-European, Hattusas.

The Far-Trading Phoenicians: Who were the Phoenicians and what was the extent of their trade? How were they alike and different from their Near East neighbors? What was the impact of the Phoenicians on culture? Identify: Tyrean purple, Byblos, Tyre, Sidon, Carthage.

THE HEBREWS: What is monotheism and how did it develop under the Hebrews?

The Wandering Years: What happened to the Hebrews during their wandering years? Identify: Palestine, Canaanites, judges, Saul, Samuel, David, Jerusalem, torah.

The Kingdom of David: What was the significance of David's rule? Identify: Saul, Israel

The Splendor of Solomon: What was the extent of Solomon's splendor? Identify: Solomon, Judea, Israel, Diaspora.

Division and Disaster: What happened after Solomon's reign? Why did Israel decline? What other groups controlled Israel?

THE BIRTH OF MONOTHEISM: How did the Hebrew understanding of Yahweh change over time? What is the significance of monotheism?

Hebrew Society: Describe Hebrew family life. How did the role of women change over time? How did the Hebrew laws intersect with a sense of identity?

The Worship of One God: What were the various elements of Hebrew faith? What elements were different from other Near Eastern religions?

The Hebrew Heritage: What is the Hebrew history? What are the foundations of the religion? Identify: Dome of the Rock, Church of the Holy Sepulcher, Wailing Wall.

SUMMARY: What are the main points of the chapter?

STUDY SKILLS EXERCISES

1. **Making Connections:** Compare the Hebrew religion to that of the Egyptians.

2. **Reflection:** Why did the Hebrew religion have such a powerful impact on the world?

3. **Timeline:** The first timeline is related to the Hebrews and other satellite cultures.

2600-2200 B.C.E.	Elba
1400-1200 B.C.E.	Hittites
1100-800 B.C.E.	Phoenicians
ca. 1300 B.C.E.	Hebrew Exodus
1020 B.C.E.	Kingdom of Israel founded
1000-922 B.C.E.	David and Solomon
8th century B.C.E.	Israel falls into Assyria
6th century B.C.E.	Judah falls to Babylonians
550-538 B.C.E.	Babylonian Captivity

4. **Maps:**
   a. **Ancient Civilizations: The Continental Crossroads: 3500-200 B.C.E.** (p. 7) Locate Israel.
   b. **The Realm of King David:** (p. 58) Where is Phoenicia? What modern day area does it correspond to? Compare ancient Israel to modern in terms of area. Locate Tyre, Sidon, Damascus, Jerusalem.
   c. **The Kingdoms of Israel and Judah, c. 800 B.C.E.** (p. 73) Compare the area of Israel to Judah. What areas had Israel lost in the north compared to David's realm?

RECITE/REVIEW

Multiple Choice

1. The patriarch of the Hebrew tribes was
   a. Moses
   b. David
   c. Nebuchadnezzar
   d. Abraham

2. The Hittites' contribution to civilization of the ancient Near East was
   a. the alphabet.   c. Zoroastrianism.
   b. iron-making.   d. gold friezes.

3. Which one of the following has the **LEAST** association with the others?
   a. Tyrean purple   c. alphabet
   b. Byblos   d. iron

4. Which one of the following was **NOT** one of the kings of Israel?
   - a. Moses
   - b. Saul
   - c. David
   - d. Solomon

5. From the beginning **THIS** Hebrew god demanded an exclusive devotion that other Near Eastern gods did not:
   - a. Ahura Mazda
   - b. Isaiah
   - c. Yahweh
   - d. Yehudim

6. The practice of marrying only with a community is known as
   - a. exogamy
   - b. monogamy
   - c. endogamy
   - d. polygamy

7. According to tradition, Moses was the author of
   - a. the *Pentateuch*
   - b. the *Tanach*
   - c. the Ten Commandments
   - d. the Book of Proverbs

8. Before unification under David, the Hebrews were led by
   - a. a single king
   - b. judges and prophets
   - c. a powerful queen
   - d. priests

9. His rule was marked by "opulent Near Eastern" palaces, temples, harems and stables
   - a. Moses
   - b. Saul
   - c. David
   - d. Solomon

10. After Solomon's death, the nation split into two parts:
    - a. Jordan and Israel
    - b. Gaza and Judea
    - c. Judea and Israel
    - d. Babylonia and Egypt

11. The *diaspora* is
    - a. the dispersal of the Hebrews throughout the Western World
    - b. the first five books of the Bible
    - c. the period of enslavement in Egypt
    - d. the captivity in Babylon

12. Among the earliest Hebrews, society was organized by
    - a. a single unified kingdom
    - b. tribe, clans and families
    - c. matriarchy
    - d. a loose confederation of the descendants of Moses

13. The Hebrews of Abraham's day saw their god as
    - a. the only real god in existence
    - b. one god among many
    - c. the ruler of other gods in a pantheon
    - d. the same god the Egyptians called Aton

Short Essay

14. What was the role of the Exodus in Hebrew history?
15. How do identity and law interact for the Hebrews?
16. How did Yahweh differ from the gods of Egypt, India, and Greece?

Extended Essay

17. Compare David to Solomon in terms of political leadership and contributions to history.
18. How did the Hebrew's view of Yahweh change over time?
19. **Making Connections:** Compare the Hebrew views of Yahweh at the time of Solomon with the Egyptian god Re.

Timeline and Maps

20. The order of kingship was
    a. Saul, Solomon, David
    b. Moses, David, Solomon
    c. Abraham, Moses, David
    d. Saul, David, Solomon

21. During the reign of David, Israel's neighbors included
    a. Phoenicia and Moab
    b. Jordan and Syria
    c. Egypt and Palestine
    d. Canaan and Hattusas

22. The temple of Solomon was destroyed in
    a. 591 B.C.E.
    b. 586 B.C.E.
    c. C.E. 1
    d. 614 B.C.E.

23. After the collapse of Solomon's kingdom, Jerusalem and Bethlehem lay in
    a. Judea
    b. Israel
    c. Moab
    d. Assyria

ANSWERS

Multiple Choice:
1. d, p. 59
2. b, pp. 57-58
3. d, pp. 57-58
4. a, p. 59
5. c, p. 62
6. c, p. 62
7. a, p. 59
8. b, p. 59
9. d, p. 60
10. c, p. 60
11. a, p. 60
12. b, p. 61
13. b, p. 62

Short Essay:
14. p. 59
15. p. 62
16. p. 63

Extended Essay:
17. pp. 59-61
18. pp. 62-63
19. Chapters 3 and 4

Timeline and Maps:
20. d, pp. 59, 64
21. a, p. 58
22. b, p. 60
23. a, p. 59

5
_____

ATHENA AND THE PHILOSOPHERS: THE GREEK CITY-STATES (1500-200 B.C.E.)

SURVEY

Chapter Overview: In Europe, ancient civilization began in the islands and mainland Greece with the Minoans, Mycenaens and the classical Greeks. Look at the outline on p. 66 and read the summary on p. 83.

Chapter Objectives:

1. Describe the basic features of Minoan and Mycenaen civilizations.
2. Compare the basic features of Minoan and Mycenaen civilizations.
3. Summarize the basic features of Minoan and Mycenaen civilizations that survived in classical Greece.
4. Describe the economic and political basis of classical Greece and explain how the geography of the area connected to them.
5. Outline the basic causes and events of external conflict with Persia and the internal conflict of the Peloponnesian War.
6. Trace the rise of Alexander and his long march to glory including the effects of his actions on the Near East.
7. Explain the contributions that make Greece the fountainhead of Western Culture.
8. **Making Connections**: Compare the culture of Greece to that of Egypt.

QUESTIONS/READ

MINOANS AND MYCENAENS: Who were the Minoans and Mycenaena? What were the main features of these cultures?

   Mountains and the Sea: What are the essential features of Greek geography and how did these affect their development? Identify: polis.

   The Minoans: Who were the Minoans and where were they based? What was the economic basis of their civilization?

   The Mycenaens: Who and where were the Mycenaens? What was their impact on the Minoans? What were the main features of Mycenaen civilization? Identify: tholos, *Illiad*.

   The Greek Dark Age: What was the Greek Dark Age? What were the features of it? Identify: Dorians, Ionians, Homer, Hesiod.

CLASSICAL GREECE: What were the basic elements of classical Greek civilization?

   Wealth and Colonies: What was the basis of Greek wealth? Why did the colonies develop and what was their extent? What cultural unity was maintained in this immigration? What products were traded? What effect did trade have on their language?

The Greek City-State: What was the significance of the Greek city-state? How was the polis connected to its citizens? How did the polis develop from its tribal beginnings? What factors contributed to the decline of the aristocracy? What was the extent of the "democracy" of the Greek city-state? How was it different from the rule of other civilizations? Identify: acropolis, hoplites, tyrants.

The Persian War: What caused the Persian war? How do Marathon and Salamis fit into the war? What Greek city-states were the most involved in the Persian War? Identify: Darius I, Xerex, Thermopylae, Themistocles, Plataea.

The Athens of Pericles: Who was Pericles and why is Athens identified with him? How did the history of Athens parallel other Greek city-states? What are the structures of participatory democracy? How did the Athenian empire develop?

Alexander the Great; Long March to Glory: Who was Alexander the Great and what was his long march to glory? What impact did Alexander's conquests have? Identify: Philip II of Macedon, Chaeronea, Gaugamela.

THE FOUNTAINHEAD OF WESTERN CULTURE: Why is Greece called the fountainhead of Western culture? What works, ideas and values became part of it?

The Art of the Acropolis: What were the themes of Greek art, both Hellenic and Hellenistic? What is the characteristic structure of early Greek architecture? Identify: head of Pericles, Aphrodite, *Old Market Woman,* Doric order.

Homer's Epics and Athenian Tragedy: What are the epics of Homer? What are the major tragedies of the Athenians? What ideals are expressed in Homer's epics and in Athenian tragedies? Identify: Sappho, Pindar, Sophocles, *Oedipus the King,* Aristophanes, *The Clouds.*

Philosophy: Socrates, Plato, Aristotle: What were the philosophical teachings of Socrates, Plato and Aristotle? Why did Socrates refer to himself as a "gladfly?" In what ways did Artistotle differ from Plato? Identify: *Dialogues,* Ideas, Forms, Absolutes, golden mean.

History and Science: What are the major contributions of the Greeks in history and science? Identify: Herodotus, Thucydides, Pythagoras, Aristotle, Euclid.

SUMMARY: What are the main points of the chapter?

STUDY SKILLS EXERCISES

1. **Making Connections:** Look at the various city-states of the ancient civilizations you have studied. What variety of development do you find? Look at your overview charts for all the civilizations to find trends, parallels and variety of human responses.

2. **Reflections:**
   a. How do you think things would have turned out if the Persians had won the Persian War?
   b. Of all the ancient civilizations you have studied (Chapters 2-5), which one would you choose to live under? Why?
   c. Hunter-gatherers usually emphasized harmony with nature yet they did participate in overkill of megafauna. How would you explain this?

3. **Timeline:**

3000-1800 B.C.E.	Palace at Knossos
2200-1500 B.C.E.	Minoans
1500-1100 B.C.E.	Mycenaens
1100-800	Greek Dark Age
850-600	Revival of city-state, trade and colonial expansion

500	Golden Age of Hellenic Greece begins
490-479	Persian War (Battles: Marathon 490, Thermopylae 480, Salamis 480, Plataea, 479)
450-429 B.C.E.	Age of Pericles
431-414 B.C.E.	Peloponnesian War
338 B.C.E.	Chaeronea-Phillip II of Macedon
336-323 B.C.E.	Alexander's empire (Battle of Gaugamela, 331)

4. **Maps:** If you are unfamiliar with the locations near Greece, make a map and label the following: Balkans, Peloponnesus, Mediterranean Sea, Ionian Sea, Aegean Sea, Asia Minor, Crete, Sicily, Black Sea, Hellespont, Troy, Bosporus.

   a. **Ancient Civilizations: The Continental Crossroads, 3500-200 B.C.E.:** (p. 7) Now that you have covered several chapters dealing with ancient civilizations, take a minute to review the map. As a review, make sure all the names and locations are familiar to you.

   b. **Ancient Greece:** (p. 68) Be able to locate Knossos, Crete, Mycenae, Troy, Sparta and Athens. What was the extent of the Greek colonial world? Where did the Persian Empire border on Greece? Locate these battle sites: Thermopylae, Salamis, Plataea, Marathon.

   c. **Alexander's Empire and the Hellenestic World:** (p. 78) What empire was Alexander trying to conquer? What river was on the eastern border of Alexander's empire? Follow the route of Alexander. Why do you think he went to Egypt first? What were the three successor states to Alexander's empire?

RECITE/REVIEW

Multiple Choice

1. The two geographical factors that most influenced the political development of Greece were the presence of
   - a. desert and sea.
   - b. plateaus and mountains.
   - c. mountains and sea.
   - d. forests and plains.

2. The basis of Minoan success was
   - a. war.
   - b. trade.
   - c. education.
   - d. technology.

3. Which one of the following has the **LEAST** connection to the others?
   - a. Linear A
   - b. Crete
   - c. Knossos
   - d. tholos

4. Homer's *Illiad* and the armada against Troy were based on the exploits of
   - a. Alexander's Macedonians.
   - b. Mycenaean warriors.
   - c. Periclean Athens.
   - d. Spartan soldiers.

5. The colonial expansion of the Greeks was largely due to
   - a. population growth.
   - b. Indo-European invasions that drove them out.
   - c. a desire for imperial conquest.
   - d. continual exploration.

6. Athenian support of the Ionian city-states in 499 B.C led to the
   - a. age of colonial expansion.
   - b. Peloponnesian War.
   - c. invasion by Philip II of Macedonia.
   - d. Persian War.

7. Which one of the following battles of the Persian War is **NOT** correctly matched to its outcome?
    a. Marathon-Athenians defeat Persians.
    b. Thermopylae-Spartans die to halt Persians.
    c. Plataea-Spartan-led unified Greeks drive back Persians.
    d. Salamis-Persians defeat Athens on the high seas.

8. Which one of the following is **NOT** part of the Athenian democracy?
    a. citizen-jury system
    b. an assembly of citizens
    c. Council of Five Hundred
    d. male and female suffrage

9. The Peloponnesian War was the result of
    a. attacks of Philip II of Macedon.
    b. interference of the Persians in Greek colonial areas.
    c. rivalry between Athens and Sparta.
    d. revolt of slaves and unrepresented people of Athens.

10. The Battle of Chaeronea marked the victory of
    a. the Spartans over the Athenians.
    b. Philip II taking control of much of Greece.
    c. Alexander's defeat of the Persian emperor, Darius II.
    d. the Greeks over the Persians.

11. Hellenic Greek sculpture at its most developed stage was characterized by a/an
    a. fixed smile and rigid frontality.
    b. idealized physical shape and proportion.
    c. violent twisted and mechanistic shapes.
    d. realism and sentiment in subjects.

12. To Plato, which one of the following was **NOT** part of pure or ultimate reality?
    a. Particulars
    b. Ideas.
    c. Forms.
    d. Absolutes.

13. Aristotle differed from Plato in
    a. being an intellectual "gadfly."
    b. seeing like as a search for truth.
    c. stressing philosophy for the ordinary mind.
    d. the relationship between Forms and particulars.

Short Essay

14. What is the significance of the geographical features of sea and mountains in Greek development?
15. To what degree would Sophocles' Oedipus embody Aristotle's idea of the perfect tragic type?
16. Who was the "father of History" and what did he do to earn that title? Pg. 82

Extended Essay

17. What was the *polis* and how was it significant to the Greeks as well as to Western Civilization?
18. Trace the development of the city-state of Athens to the establishment of the Athenian Empire. Analyze the problems the Athenians had in doing this.
19. Discuss the "legacy of daring ideas" left by Socrates, Plato and Aristotle.

Timeline and Maps

20. The heyday of Minoan Civilization basically extended from
    a. 2200-1500 B.C
    b. 1500-1100 B.C
    c. 1100-800 B.C
    d. 850-600 B.C

31

21. The Golden Age of Hellenic Greece began approximately by
    a. 2200-1500 B.C
    b. 1500-1100 B.C
    c. 1100-800 B.C
    d. 850-600 B.C

22. Which one of the following is in the correct chronological order?
    a. Greek colonial expansion, Persian War, Age of Pericles, Peloponnesian War
    b. Greek colonial expansion, Age of Pericles, Peloponnesian War, Persian War
    c. Persian War, Peloponnesian War, Age of Pericles, Greek colonial expansion
    d. Peloponnesian War, Age of Pericles, Greek colonial expansion, Persian War

23. Which one of the following is in the correct chronological order?
    a. Gaugemela, Chaeronia, Plataea, Marathon
    b. Chaeronia, Marathon, Plataea, Gaugemela
    c. Marathon, Plataea, Gaugemela, Chaeronia
    d. Marathon, Plataea, Chaeronia, Gaugemela

24. The Minoan city of Knossos was located on the
    a. island of Sicily.
    b. coast of Ionia.
    c. island of Crete.
    d. Peloponneus.

25. Which one of the following was **NOT** part of the Greek colonial world?
    a. coasts of France and Spain
    b. around the Black Sea
    c. Sicily and southern Italy
    d. old site of Carthage

26. Alexander's eastern border reached to the
    a. Tigris River.
    b. Indus River.
    c. Black Sea.
    d. Persian Gulf.

ANSWERS

Multiple Choice
1. c, p. 67
2. b, p. 67
3. d, p. 70
4. b, p. 70
5. a, p. 71
6. d, p. 73
7. d, p. 74
8. d, pp. 74-75
9. c, p. 76
10. b, p. 76
11. b, p. 78
12. a, pp. 81-82
13. d, p. 82

Short Essay:
14. p. 67
15. pp. 80-82
16. p. 82

Extended Essay:
17. pp. 71-73
18. pp. 74-76
19. pp. 80-82

Timeline and Maps:
20. a, p. 69
21. c, p. 71
22. a, pp. 71-76
23. d, pp. 73-76
24. c, p. 67
25. d, p. 71
26. b, p. 77

OVERVIEW II

ANCIENT CIVILIZATIONS: THE FARTHER REACHES, (2500-200 B.C.E)

This overview sets the stage for Chapters 6 through 10. Do not skip these overviews as they will help tie together the sections of the text and the book as a whole.

Questions:
1. What does the author mean by "the farther reaches"?
2. What connections existed between the Crossroads and the Farther Reaches?
3. What differences and similarities existed between the various cultures.

Map: Ancient Civilizations: The Farther Reaches, 2500-200 B.C.E. (p. 87).

COMPARISON CHART FOR OVERVIEW II:
ANCIENT CIVILIZATIONS: THE FARTHER REACHES.
Photocopy this chart so you can use it for chapters 6-10 (you need at least 5 copies)

THEMES AND PATTERNS OF CIVILIZATIONS	CIVILIZATION_____ (fill in name)
Geographic and/or historic setting (include major cities)	
Government(s) (include major leaders)	
Society (include class issue, roles of women)	
Economy (growth of trade-include major cities, goods and extent of trade)	
Science and Technology	
Literacy, writing, literature	
Arts	
Ideas and Values (include religion, philosophy, political ideals)	

TIMELINE: Photocopy this page as you will need at least one timeline for most of the chapters.

CHAPTER TITLE _____

| ____ | ____ | ____ | ____ | ____ | ____ | ____ | ____ | ____ | ____ | ____ | ____ |_

CHAPTER TITLE _____

| ____ | ____ | ____ | ____ | ____ | ____ | ____ | ____ | ____ | ____ | ____ | ____ |_

CHAPTER TITLE _____

| ____ | ____ | ____ | ____ | ____ | ____ | ____ | ____ | ____ | ____ | ____ | ____ |_

CHAPTER TITLE _____

| ____ | ____ | ____ | ____ | ____ | ____ | ____ | ____ | ____ | ____ | ____ | ____ |_

CHAPTER TITLE _____

| ____ | ____ | ____ | ____ | ____ | ____ | ____ | ____ | ____ | ____ | ____ | ____ |_

6

BRAHMAN AND LORD BUDDHA: THE RISE OF INDIAN CIVILIZATION (2500-200 B.C.E.)

SURVEY

Chapter Overview: India developed ancient civilizations based in the cities located on the Indus and Ganges Rivers. See chapter outline on p. 88. Read the summary on p. 101.

Chapter Objectives:

1. Describe the basic geographic elements of India.
2. Describe and compare early civilizations of the Indus and Ganges.
3. Trace the changes in Indian society from the Aryan invasions to the rise of the Mauryas.
4. Summarize the accomplishments of the Maurya dynasty.
5. Outline the accomplishments of arts and literature in the cities of India.
6. Trace the major ideas of Hinduism.
7. Summarize the major ideas of Buddhism and compare them to Hinduism.
8. **Making Connections:** Your author points out that the Indians were as profoundly religious as the ancient Egyptians and Hebrews. Compare the beliefs of these three civilizations.

QUESTIONS/READ

LOST CIVILIZATION OF THE INDUS: Why is the civilization referred to as "lost?" What has been discovered about it?

The Indian Subcontinent: What are the geographical subdivisions of the Indian subcontinent? What are the monsoons and how do they affect India?

Harappan Culture: What were the characteristics of Harappan culture? Where was it located? What other city was part of Harappan culture? What contacts did they have with others?

The Aryan Invasions: Who were the Aryans and what did they invade? What caused the invasion? What happened to the Harappans? Identify: Hindu Vedas, Idra, Purandara.

KINGDOMS OF THE GANGES: What were the kingdoms of the Ganges? What was their extent? What were their characteristics?

Cities in the Jungle: How did the Aryan cities develop out of the jungle? Where did the Aryans migrate with India? Identify: Aryan-Dravidian synthesis, Patna, Benares.

Social Structure: From Color Bar to Caste: How did the caste structure develop? What was its association with color? What other bases were there to these divisions? What were the rules and sanctions of caste? How was it both rigid and tolerant? Identify: varna, kshatriyas, Brahmans, vaisyas, sudras, "untouchables."

The Rise of the Rajas: Who were the rajas and how did they rise to power? What two new forms of state developed in northern India? What was the religious political connection? What was Magadha and what was its significance to India's future? What was its geographical orientation? Identify: Nandes.

The Mauryas Chandragupta: Who were the Mauryas and what was the significance of Chanragupta? What was the extent of the Maurya empire? What was the scope of their achievement? Identify: Kautilya, Seleucus, Bindusara.

Asoka, the Philosopher King: Who was Asoka and why was he called the philospher king? What religion did he promote? What were his principles? How did it affect his governing? Identify: Kaligna, dharma, ahimsa, Grand Trunk Road.

THE SOUL OF INDIA: What various arts and ideas make up the soul of India?

The Lost Arts of Ancient India: Why were many of the arts lost? What survived? What are the themes and styles of what survived? Identify: yakshas, yakshis.

Epic Poetry: The Song of God: What are the major epic poems of Ancient Indian civilization? What is the *Song of God?* What are the themes of the *Mahabharata* and the *Ramayana*? What is the *Arthasastra* and what ideas are expressed in it? Identify: Vishnu, Brahman, *Bhagavadgita*, Arnuna, Krishna, Rama, Diwali.

Hinduism: From the Sacred Cow to Brahman: What are the basic beliefs of Hinduism? What works form the core of Hindu scripture? How did Hinduism merge and evolve from Dravidians and Aryans? Who were the most popular gods of Hinduism: Who are the most important? Identify: Rama, Sita, Krishna, Brahma, Vishnu, Shiva, Brahman, *Upanishads*, karma, ashima, maya.

The Naked Philosophers: Who were the "naked philosophers" and what were their ideas? How were the gymnodophists a new view in Hinduism: Which gurus became the most important? Identify: Mahavira, Janis, ashisma.

Buddhism: The Teachings of Prince Siddartha: Who was Prince Siddartha and what were his teachings? How did his teachings compare to Hinduism? What is Nirvana and how does one attain it? What Asian areas were affected by Buddhism? Identify: Buddha, Sarnath.

SUMMARY: What are the major points in this chapter?

STUDY SKILLS EXERCISES

1. **Making connections:** a. Compare Rama and Sita in Hinduism to Osiris and Isis in Egyptian religion. b. Compare Asoka to Akhenaton in terms of religious leadership.

2. **Reflection:** Why do you think religion played such a strong role in the Indian, Egyptian and Hebrew cultures?

3. **Timeline:**

2500-1500 B.C.E.	Harappan Culture
1500 B.C.E.	Beginning of Aryan Invasion
1500-500 B.C.E.	Aryan predominance
1000-500 B.C.E.	Aryan-Dravidian Synthesis
1000 B.C.E.	Rise of Hinduism
500 B.C.E.	Rise of the Rajas
500 B.C.E.	Upanishadic times
321-185 B.C.E.	Mauryan dynasty
563-483 B.C.E.	Prince Siddartha

4. **Maps:**
a. **Early Civilizations of the Indus and Ganges:** (p. 90) Explain the importance of the Indus and Ganges to the civilizations of India.

RECITE/REVIEW

Multiple Choice

1. Which one of the following is **NOT** a geographic feature of the Indian subcontinent?
   - a. Steppes
   - b. Deccan
   - c. Ganges
   - d. Himalayas

2. The monsoons are
   - a. typhoon-like storms.
   - b. seasonal winds that bring a rainy season.
   - c. meltwaters from the Hindu Kush and Himalayas.
   - d. high icy plateaus that cover much of northern India.

3. Our knowledge of Harappan culture is based mainly on
   - a. translation of literacy texts since there are few ruins.
   - b. epic poems and mythological texts of early Hinduism.
   - c. chronicles by later Mauryan historians.
   - d. archaeological excavation of impressive ruins.

4. Which one of the following is **NOT** true of the Harappans?
   - a. They had contact with the outside world.
   - b. Their cities were well-planned.
   - c. Centralized authority seemed to be present.
   - d. They had irrigation systems like those of Mesopotamia.

5. Following the Harappans, a new civilization developed along the
   - a. Ganges
   - b. Deccan.
   - c. Arabian Sea.
   - d. Hindu Kush.

6. The Indian word for caste was varna meaning
   - a. class.
   - b. occupation.
   - c. color.
   - d. society.

7. The two new forms of state that emerged in early northern India were
   - a. republics and kingdoms.
   - b. city state and villages.
   - c. empires and monarchies.
   - d. class and tribes.

8. Changragupta was the builder of this empire:
   - a. Harappan
   - b. Magadhan
   - c. Mauryan
   - d. Dravidian

9. Asoka advocated the Indian virtue of ahimsa or
   - a. saving truth of Buddha.
   - b. non-violence.
   - c. fate.
   - d. tolerance.

10. Most arts of ancient India were destroyed. Much of what is known is based on city patterns, carved seals, and nature spirit figures called
    - a. dotis.
    - b. yakshas.
    - c. sudras.
    - d. Kshatriyas.

11. Which one of the following is **NOT** one of the early works of Indian literature?
    - a. *Ramayana*
    - b. *Mahabharata*
    - c. *Arthasastra*
    - d. *Karma*

12. These three gods were aspects of the universal Hindu spiritual principle:
    a. Brahma, Vishnu, Shiva
    b. Veda, Unpanished, Bhagavadgita
    c. Rama, Krihna, Kali
    d. Indra, Agni, Varuna

13. The most significant of gurus or gymnosophists from the 6th century B.C.E. were
    a. Brahman and Kshatriya
    b. Ramayana and Krishna
    c. Gautama and Asoka
    d. Mahavira and Siddartha

14. The Buddha and orthodox Hindus accepted this idea that worldly things are a grand illusion:
    a. maya.
    b. karma.
    c. dharma.
    d. nirvana.

Short Essay

15. What is the significance of Indra, the Aryan war god, styling himself as Purandara?
16. What is the Aryan-Dravidian synthesis?
17. Compare the goal of a Hindu with the goal of a Buddhist.

Extended Essay

18. Describe the Mauryan Dynasty and the Golden Age of Asoka.
19. Compare the empire building of Chandragupta and his advisor Kautilya to that of Asoka.
20. Compare the major ideas of Hinduism to Buddhism in these early years. Include a discussion of the connections between the two religions.

Timeline and Maps

21. The ancient Indian civilization called Harappan lasted from
    a. 2500-1500 B.C.E.
    b. 2000 B.C.E.
    c. 1000-500 B.C.E..
    d. 500 B.C.E.

22. The Aryan-Dravidian synthesis and the rise of Hinduism began by
    a. 3000 B.C.E.
    b. 2000 B.C.E.
    c. 1000-500 B.C.E.
    d. 500 B.C.E.

23. Which one of the following has the events in the correct order?
    a. Mauryan dynasty, Aryan invasion, Harappans, Buddha
    b. Buddha, Harappans, Aryan invasion Mauryan dynasty
    c. Harappans, Aryan invasion, Maryan dynasty, Buddha
    d. Aryan invasion, Harappans, Buddha, Muaryan dynasty

24. This empire managed to cover most of India by 185 B.C.E.
    a. Harappan
    b. Indus
    c. Ganges State
    d. Mauryan

25. Which one of the following has the **LEAST** in common with the other three?
    a. Magadha
    b. Indus
    c. Harappa
    d. Mohenjo-Daro

26. Harappan civilization is in the modern-day country of
    a. Afghanistan.
    b. Pakistan.
    c. India.
    d. Sri Lanka.

27. The Tigris and Euphrates were to Mesopotamia as these were to India:
    a. Thar and Deccan
    b. Indus and Ganges
    c. India.
    d. Harappa and Mohenjo

ANSWERS

Multiple Choice:
1. a, p. 89
2. b, p. 89
3. d, p. 89
4. d, p. 91
5. a, p. 92
6. c, p. 93
7. a, p. 93
8. c, p. 94
9. b, p. 96
10. b, p. 98
11. d, p. 98
12. a, p. 99
13. d, p. 100
14. a, p. 100

Short Essay:
15. p. 92
16. p. 93
17. pp. 99-101

Extended Essay:
18. pp. 94-97
19. pp. 94-97
20. pp. 99-101

Timeline and Maps:
21. a, p. 89
22. c, p. 93
23. c, pp. 89-99
24. d, p. 94
25. a, pp. 89, 94
26. b, p. 89
27. b, p. 89

7 _____

THE AGE OF THE SAGES: THE RISE OF THE CHINESE CIVILIZATION (1500-200 B.C.E.)

SURVEY

Chapter Overview: Ancient civilization in China was formed by the Shang, Zhou and Qin dynasties. Look at the chapter outline on p. 103 and read the summary on p. 116.

Chapter Objectives: After reading this chapter and following SQ3r, you should be able to:

1. List the main features of the early Shang culture and its legacy to China's development.
2. Describe the structure of the Zhou and Chinese feudal system.
3. Summarize the accomplishments of the Qin dynasty.
4. Describe the major objects and motifs of art in this early period.
5. Describe the major elements of early Chinese literature.
6. List and compare the ideas of Confucians, Daoists and Legalists.
7. **Making Connections:** Compare the various methods by which rulers and the ruling class used religious concepts to justify their rule.

QUESTIONS/READ

SHANG CULTURE: Where and when did Shang culture exits? What contributions did it make to Chinese history?

The Middle Kingdom of East Asia: What does the term "Middle Kingdom" mean? What are the main geographical elements of China? How does modern China compare to the U.S. in size? Identify: Huanghe River, Yangzi River.

From Prehistory to History: How did the shift from prehistory to history occur in China? What is the significance of sculpumancy to writing? What practice was a precursor to veneration of ancestors?

The Shang State: What social classes existed under the Shang state? What was its political organization?

Families, Cities, Culture: What was the role of the family in Chinese society, and what was its structure? What were the major features of cities under the Shang? How did ancestor worship develop and who practiced it? Identify: Shangdi , Tian.

THE ZHOU DYNASTY AND CHINESE FEUDALISM: What are the major accomplishments of the Zhou dynasty? What was the structure of Chinese feudalism?

The Kings of the Western Zhou: Who were the kings of the Western Zhou? What was their contribution to Chinese civilization? What was the size of their empire? Identify: Duke of Zhou, sons of Heaven, King Wu.

Zhou Feudalism: How did the Zhou feudal state work and how was it justified? What was the concept of the Mandate of Heaven?

The Eastern Zhou: Progress in a World at War: Why did the Zhou shift from west to east? What was the result politically? How did China improve during this period? Identify: warring states, copper "cash," shi.

THE QIN DYNASTY UNIFIES CHINA: How did the Qin dynasty unify China? What was the effect of this unity?

The Rise of the House of Qin: Where was the House of Qin and how did they rise to power? What were the elements of the philosophy of Legalism in practice? Identify: Li Si, Qin Shi Huangdi.

Shi Huangdi: The First Emperor of China: What areas of China were controlled by Shi Huangdi? What type of rule did he establish? How did it help unify the empire?

The Man Who Built the Great Wall of China: What is the Great Wall of China and to what extent did the First Emperor build it? What other building projects did the First Emperor embark on and what was their effect? What happened to his empire when he died? What did he contribute to his empire when he died? What did he contribute to China's unity?

ART AND THOUGHT OF ANCIENT CHINA: What were the basic features and ideas of art and thought in ancient China?

Art: Bronze Dragons and Clay Soldiers: What are the main types of art that have survived from China's early history? What were the elements of the bronze vessels? Who were the clay soldiers? What was the significance of the tomb of the First Emperor at Xi'an?

Literature: Chinese Characters and the *Book of Songs*: What are the significant features of Chinese characters? How did it limit literacy but help unify China? Identify: oracle bones, *Book of Songs*.

The Sages: The Teachings of Confucius: What were the concerns of Chinese sages? Who was Confucius and what were his main teachings? Identify: "Master Kong," *Analects?*

The Hundred Flowers: What were the "hundred flowers?" What were the ideas of the three major groups: Confucians, Legalists and Daoists? Identify: Mencius, Han Faizi, Laozi, *Daodejing,* Dao.

SUMMARY: What are the main points of this chapter?

STUDY SKILLS EXERCISES

1. **Making Connections:** What is the similarity between the ideas of the Legalists such as Han Faizi and those of Kautilya in his *Arthastra* (Chapter 6)?

2. **Reflection:** Whose advice for a good life sounds the most useful or appealing to you: that of Confucius, Laozi or Han Faizi? Which one of their views of human nature do you think is closest to yours?

3. **Timeline:**

1500-1000 B.C.E.	Shang Dynasty
1000-221 B.C.E.	Zhous Dynasty
ca. 400-221 B.C.E.	Warring States Period
221-206 B.C.E.	Qin Dynasty

4. **Maps**: If you are unfamiliar with the geography of China, trace an outline of China and locate the following: Gobi Desert, Pamir Mts., Himalayan Mts, Pacific Ocean, Huanghe River, Beijing, Yanzi, Guangzhou, Hong Kong, Tibet, Xinjiang.
   a. **Ancient Civilizations: The Farther Reaches, 2500-200 B.C.E:** (p. 87) Describe the general locations of the Shang, Zhou and Qin China.
   b. **China in the Shang, Zhou and Qin Dynasties:** (p. 105) What rivers are the Shang, Zhou and Qin centered on ? Where is the Great Wall?

RECITE/REVIEW

Multiple Choice

1. Which of the following is NOT true of Chinese geography?
   a. The Huanghe River of the north has been the political center.
   b. The Yanzi River marks the fertile area of central China.
   c. The south is the driest and poorest commercial area of China.
   d. It is slightly larger than the United States.

2. China viewed itself as the Middle Kingdom" which meant the middle of
   a. trade for Asia.
   b. civilization surrounded by barbarians.
   c. religious and philosophical leadership.
   d. warring states.

3. From the early Neolithic Villages, we find practices of careful burial and of sculpumancy which were precursors of ancestor veneration and
   a. writing.
   b. bronze vessels.
   c. feudalism.
   d. astrology.

4. The political structure of the Shang dynasty was basically
   a. feudal.
   b. a loose confederation of clan states.
   c. an empire based on provinces.
   d. a small democratic city-state.

5. In terms of social class, the practice of ancestor worship under the Shang
   a. equalized social ranking.
   b. justified the caste system.
   c. gave ruling advantage to the aristocracy.
   d. made the king divine.

6. Zhou China was essentially a
   a. city state.
   b. democracy.
   c. feudal state.
   d. theocracy.

7. Which one of the following is NOT a claim the Zhou rulers made under the Mandate of Heaven?
   a. a divine charge to govern their lands
   b. a rationalization for their rule
   c. a cosmic pattern of interrupted harmony and reestablished order
   d. a divinity for the emperor like the Egyptian pharaoh

8. Which one of the following is NOT true of the Eastern Zhou?
   a. A period of division called the Warring states was experienced.
   b. China became the most populous civilization in the world.
   c. Great economic and cultural growth occurred.
   d. The society became rigid and stratified.

9. Of the legacies of the First Emperor, the ones that most lived on are
   a. the Great Wall and China's unity.
   b. bronze vessels and Confucian ways.
   c. ancestor worship and the Mandate of Heaven.
   d. a consistent spoken and written language.

10. The best preserved arts of China are its
   - a. royal palaces of the Shang, Zhou and Qin.
   - b. bronze ritual vessels and the terra cotta soldiers.
   - c. elaborate gardens of the Zhou.
   - d. copper and bronze "cash" coins and ritual masks.

11. The prestige of the scholar and the great power of the governmental administrators was partly due to
   - a. Legalist doctrines of need for ruthless centralized power.
   - b. weak rulers under a feudal structure.
   - c. the difficulty of learning to write the Chinese language.
   - d. their being viewed as the "Middle Kingdom" of power.

12. Chinese philosophers were most concerned with
   - a. abstract truth.
   - b. logic.
   - c. mystical experience.
   - d. human relations.

13. To Confucius, the primary concern of Chinese rulers should be
   - a. autocratic control.
   - b. care of the people
   - c. a strong military.
   - d. developing trade and agriculture.

Short Essay

14. Explain what *shi* is and what it could gain for you under the Zhou.
15. What does the *Book of Songs* tell us about ancient China?
16. When Mao Zedong took control of China, he briefly tried to open up his closed society with the slogan "Let a Hundred Flowers Bloom." What Chinese legacy was he trying to use to his advantage in the 20th century?

Extended Essay

17. Trace the rise of the House of Qin and the accomplishments of Shi Huangdi.
18. Compare the views of the Legalists, Confucians and Daoists on human nature and attaining of the good life.
19. Chinese rulers wanted the Mandate of Heaven. In modern democracies, parties want the mandate of the people. Analyze the strengths and weaknesses of the Chinese approach.

Timeline and Maps

20. The earliest of Chinese civilizations saw the Shang dynasty which extended from
   - a. 1500-1000 B.C.E.
   - b. 1000-221 B.C.E.
   - c. 4th-3rd centuries B.C.E.
   - d. 321-306 B.C.E.

21. Both the Western and Eastern Zhou governed China from
   - a. 1500-1000 B.C.E.
   - b. 1000-221 B.C.E.
   - c. 4th-3rd centuries B.C.E.
   - d. 523-306 B.C.E.

22. The First Emperor Shi Huangdi governed and unified China during his reign from
   - a. 1530-1480 B.C.E.
   - b. 1089-999 B.C.E.
   - c. 551-526 B.C.E.
   - d. 221-206 B.C.E.

23. The earliest Chinese civilization, the Shang, centered on what river?
   - a. Huanghe
   - b. Yangzi
   - c. Wei
   - d. Pearl

24. To hold back barbarian invaders, the Great Wall of China was built. It runs mainly
    a. east and west in the northern part of China.
    b. north and south along the eastern coast of China.
    c. east and west in the southern part of China and Tibet.
    d. north and south in the lands of the Western Zhou.

25. Modern China is approximately the same size as
    a. the former Soviet Union.   c. India.
    b. the United States.   d. ancient Egypt.

26. China's commercial center has historically been in the
    a. western crossroads.   c. same area as the Great Wall.
    b. south coastal.   d. Yangzi area.

ANSWERS

Multiple Choice:
1. c, p. 104
2. b, p. 104
3. a, p. 104
4. b, p. 106
5. c, pp. 106-07
6. c, p. 107-08
7. d, p. 108
8. d, p. 108
9. a, p. 111
10. b, pp. 112-13
11. c, p. 113
12. d, p. 115
13. b, p. 115

Short Essay:
14. p. 108
15. pp. 114-15
16. pp. 115-16

Extended Essay:
17. pp. 109-11
18. pp. 109, 115-16
19. total chapter

Timeline and Maps:
20. a, p. 106
21. b, p. 107
22. d, pp. 109-11
23. a, p. 106
24. a, pp. 105, 111
25. b, p. 104
26. b, p. 104

8
_____

AFRICAN TRADERS AND EMPIRE BUILDERS: NUBIA AND CARTHAGE (1500-150 B.C.E.)

SURVEY

Chapter Overview: Following Egypt as the oldest African civilization were Kush, Meroe and Carthage as part of the Ancient Civilizations. Look at the outline on p. 118 and read the chapter summary on p. 126.

Chapter Objectives: After reading this chapter and following the study method recommended, you should be able to:
1. Describe the varied features of African geography.
2. Describe the varied peoples of Africa.
3. Trace the connections between Kush and Egypt.
4. Summarize the major elements of the Nubian kingdoms of Kerma, Kush and Menroe.
5. Discuss the economic, political and religious characteristics of the Carthaginian state.
6. **Making Connections:** Illustrate the connections both Kush and Carthage had with other areas of Africa, Europe and Asia.

QUESTIONS/READ

AFRICA: SOUTH AND WEST: What myths surround Africa? What diverse peoples lived in Africa?

The Second Largest Continent: What is the size of Africa relative to other continents? What types of vegetation are there? What are the bands of Africa's geography? How has the geography affected Africa's history? What varieties of people are there? How did Africa make crucial contributions to the human story before civilization's development? To what extent was Africa connected to other areas? How do the "wazungu lies" compare to reality? Identify: "dark continent," Bantu, Nubia, Kush, Carthage.

Early Contributions: How were Nubia, Kush and Carthage linked to other areas of the world? What factors explain the longevity of the "dark continent" myth?

NUBIA, KUSH AND INNER AFRICA: What were the locations of Nubia, Kush and inner Africa in terms of civilizations? What were the three Nubian kingdoms?

The Nubian Corridor: Where was the Nubian corridor and why was it a significant location? What modern day area is Nubia in? What were the three Nubian kingdoms?

The Kingdom of Kush: Where was the kingdom og Kush and how did it rise to power? What connections were there between Kush and Egypt? Identify: Kashta, Piankhi, twenty-fifth dynasty.

The Furnaces of Menroe: What was Meroe and what were the furnaces? What advantages did Meroe have? Why do we know less about Kush? Why did Kush decline and who finally conquered it?

CARTHAGE: THE EMPIRE OF THE WESTERN SEAS: where was Carthage and what was its basis of civilization?

The Phoenician Diaspora: What was the Phoenician Diaspora? When did it take place and what are the modern-day locations? What was the reason for establishing Carthage? Identify: Pillars of Hercules, Gades.

Peoples of the Magherb: Who were the peoples of the Magherb? How did they connect to the Cathaginians? Identify: Libyans, Ammon.

The Carthaginian Empire: When did the Carthaginian Empire flourish? What areas did the empire include? What was the economic basis of the empire? Identify: Numidia, Mauritania, "silent trade", Hanno.

Rivals of the Greeks and Romans: What was the nature of the rivalry between Carthage and both Greece and Rome: What were the three Punic Wars and their results? Identify: sufets, tophet, Hannibal Scipio.

SUMMARY: What were the main points of this chapter?

STUDY SKILLS

1. **Study Tip:** When you develop your maps, you should reinforce your knowledge by asking yourself the importance of each location that you place on the map. Why is this particular city, river or other location significant in this chapter? Following this practice is another way to reinforce and review material.

2. **Making Connections:** What are the bases of success of the various civilizations you have studied and what are the causes of decline?

3. **Reflection:** In several cases we have written languages that have not yet been translated such as the Kushite writing. What would be the problems of trying to determine what a civilization is like from the archaeological records? Imagine having U.S. coins and nothing else about American culture. What could you tell and what would you have to be cautious about hypothesizing?

4. **Timeline:** Put the following events on the time line below. For clarity, put the Kushite events above and the Carthaginian events below.

1100 B.C.E.	Independence of Kush
750 B.C.E.	Kushite rule of Egypt
3rd to 1st century B.C.E.	Golden Age of Kush- Meroe
800 B.C.E.	beginning of Carthage
400 B.C.E.	voyages of Hanno
5th-4th centuries B.C.E.	Carthage fought Greece
34d to 2nd centuries B.C.E.	Punic Wars with Rome

5. **Maps:** If you are not very familiar with African locations, make a map of Africa that also show the southern part of Europe and the western part of Asia. Label the following locations: Mediterranean Sea, Congo River, Nile River, Guinea Coast, Kalahari Desert, Great Rift Valley, Red Sea, Indian Ocean, Arabia, border between modern Egypt and Sudan, Aswan High Dam, Khartoum, Ethiopian Highlands, Blue and White Nile, Tyre, Lebanon, Tunisia, Atlantic Ocean, Straits of Gibraltar, Spain, Corsica, Sicily, Italy, Cameroon.
   a. **Map: Ancient Civilizations: The Farther Reaches, 2500-200 B.C.E. (p. 87)** Be able to describe the locations of Egypt, Kush and the Carthaginian Empire.
   b. **Map: Ancient Civilizations of Africa: (p. 119)** Describe the locations of Kush, Meroe, and the empire of Carthage.

   What other areas or civilizations were they close to? Explain how the map shows Africa was not cut off or isolated somehow from other civilizations. Looking at the outline of Africa and of the Arabian Peninsula, construct an argument for including the latter in the continent of Africa instead of Asia.

RECITE/REVIEW

Multiple Choice

1. Two-fifths of Africa is
    a. jungle.
    b. forest.
    c. tropical rain forest.
    d. grassy plains.

2. Which one of the following is **NOT** one of the east-west bands of African geography?
    a. fertile Mediterranean coast
    b. the Sahara Desert
    c. the Great Rift Valley
    d. sudannic belt of grassy plains

3. The population of ancient Africa was
    a. as varied as any other continent.
    b. Bantu-speaking.
    c. isolated from other areas of civilization.
    d. sparse and scattered.

4. Cheikh Anta Diop disagreed with the author about
    a. the chronological relationship between Nubian and Egyptian civilization.
    b. the significance of pyramids to Nubians and Egyptians.
    c. the beauty of Egyptian art.
    d. the relationship between Greece and Nubia.

5. Which one of the following was **NOT** an indigenous Nubian Kingdom?
    a. Meore
    b. Libya
    c. Kush
    d. all of the above

6. There were extensive connections between Kush and
    a. Phoenicia.
    b. Assyria.
    c. Mesotopia.
    d. Egypt.

7. Kings Kashta and Piankhi
    a. were Kushites who conquered Egypt.
    b. sponsored extensive voyages and explorations of Africa.
    c. were Carthaginians who conquered Numidia and Mauritania.
    d. ruled Meroe in its golden age.

8. Some Africans call this city the Birmingham or Pittsburgh of the continent:
    a. Carthage
    b. Kerma
    c. Meroe
    d. Axum

9. The Kingdom of Carthage was located in what it today the country of
    a. Tunisia.
    b. Lebanon.
    c. Sudan.
    d. Italy.

10. Carthage dominated the trade of the
    a. Nubian corridor.
    b. western Mediterranean.
    c. Near East.
    d. Greeks and Romans.

11. The famous "silent trade" of Africa had to do with
    a. slaves.
    b. iron.
    c. silver.
    d. gold.

12. The people that defeated the Carthaginians in the Punic Wars were the
      a. Romans.   c. Assyrians.
      b. Greeks.   d. Axumites.

13. If you held the position of sufet in ancient Carthage, you were a
      a. high priest.   c. ruling magistrate.
      b. merchant and trader.   d. general.

Short Essay:

14. What did the Kushnite and Carthaginian Kingdoms have in common in terms of economics?
15. What was the significance of the twenty-fifty dynasty of Egypt?

Extended Essay

16. Discuss the myth and reality of Africa as a "dark continent."
17. Compare Kush and Carthage in terms of geography, economics and politics including their relationships with other powerful kingdoms.
18. In the "Probing the Past" section of Chapter 8, your author presented the view of Senegalese scholar Cheikh Anta Diop. Discuss the evidence to support Diop's view as well as the text view.

Timeline and Maps

19. The simplified east to west geographical division of Arfica into 5 bands is complicated by
      a. the Sahara.   c. the Congo River.
      b. rain forests.   d. the Nile and Great Rift Valley.

20. The Golden Age of Kush centered around Meroe was from
      a. 1100 to 800 B.C.E.   c. 3rd to 1st century B.C.E.
      b. 800 to 500 B.C.E.   d. 1st to 4th century C.E.

21. The two major areas of civilization in Africa were in
      a. North Africa and the Sudan.   c. West Africa.
      b. South Africa.   d. Congo and Guinea coast.

ANSWERS

Multiple Choice:
1. d, p. 119
2. c, p. 119
3. a, p. 119
4. a, p. 121
5. b, pp. 120, 122
6. d, pp. 120-21
7. a, pp. 121-22
8. c, p. 122
9. a, p. 124
10. b, p. 123
11. d, p. 125
12. a, pp. 125-26
13. c, p. 125

Short Essay:
14. pp. 122, 124-25
15. pp. 121-22

Extended Essay:
16. total chapter
17. pp. 120-26
18. total chapter

Timeline and Maps:
19. d, p. 119
20. c, p. 122
21. a, p. 119

9

AMERICA'S FIRST CIVILIZATIONS: THE OLMECS AND CHAVÍN CULTURE (1500-400 B.C.E.)

SURVEY

Chapter Overview: The Ancient cultures of the Americas were the Olmecs and Chavín of the first millenium B.C.E. Look at the chapter outline on p. 128 and read the summary on p. 135.

Chapter Objectives:

1. Describe the early life of the first North Americans.
2. Summarize the features of the Olmec culture.
3. Summarize the features of the Chavín Culture.
4. Compare the Olmec and Chavín cultures.
5. **Making Connections:** Describe the various patterns of development in the cultures you have studied to date.

QUESTIONS/READ

THE FIRST NORTH AMERICANS: Who were the first North Americans? What were the major features of their societies?

The Americas Before Columbus: What are the significant geographical factors of the Americas? How were the Americas different from the other three continents studied to date? In what modern day countries did the earliest civilizations develop?

Hunters and Farmers: How did the environment affect hunting and farming in North America? As the environment changed, what was the response of Native Americans? In what areas did the life of the hunting band continue? Where did agriculture develop? What were the major crops?

Regional Economies and Family Structures: What were the different regional economies of North America? How did these economies connect to the environment? What types of gender and family relationships developed? Identify: "Fulsome points".

Harmony with Nature: What were the concepts involved in harmony with nature? What evidence is crucial in determining the ways of hunter-gatherers?

MEXICO: THE OLMECS: Who were the Olmecs? What were the major features of their civilization?

Origins of the Olmecs: What was the origin of Olmecs? Where did this civilization develop? What Old World pattern was duplicated? Identify: Middle America.

Olmec Culture: What were the features of Olmec culture? What type of art has been found and what are its features? What other type of works have been found and what are the motifs? Identify: Veracruz, La Venta.

Olmec Society: What do we know about Olmec society? What are some of the theories about political structure, religion and economics?

PERU: CHAVÍN CULTURE: What are the essential features of Chavín culture in Peru?

Origins of the Chavín Culture: What type of lands did Chavín culture develop in? What modern day countries did the civilization cover? What pattern of development occurred?

Ruins in the Andes: What is Chavín de Huantar and what does it reveal? What was terracing and what was its significance?

Chavín Reglion and Art: What do we know about Chavín religion and art? How does it compare to Olmec? Identify: Castillo.

SUMMARY: What are the main points of the chapter?

STUDY SKILLS EXERCISES

1. **Making Connections:** What common Old World patterns of development from hunter-gatherer to civilization were followed by the peoples of the Americas?

2. **Reflections:**
   a. Cats, especially jaguars, were a major element of religion and art in Olmec and Chavín cultures. What might be some explanations for this?
   b. Neither Olmec or Chavín developed along major rivers as did many of the other cultures you have studied. Consider various explanations for this.
   c. Hunter-gatherers usually emphasized harmony with nature yet they did participate in overkill of megafauna. How would you explain this?

3. **Timeline**:

1540-400 B.C.E.	Olmecs
800-400 B.C.E.	Highpoint of Olmec Art
800-400 B.C.E.	Chavín

4. **Maps:**
   a. If you are not familiar with the geography of the Americas, make yourself a map and locate the following: North, South and Central America, Rockies, Andes, Caribbean, Cape Horn, Canadian tundra, Argentine Pampas, Gran Chaco, Patagonia, Bering Strait, Rio Grande, Great Lakes, Yucatán Peninsula, Amazon, Cordillera Blanca, Atlantic and Pacific Oceans. Know where these modern day countries are: Canada, United States, Mexico, Guatemala, Honduras, Peru, Bolivia, Ecuador, Chile, Argentina.
   b. **Ancient Civilizations: The Farther Reaches, 2500-200 B.C.E.:** (p. 87) In what areas or modern day countries are the Olmec and Chavín cultures located?
   c. **Ancient American Civilizations:** (p. 129) Locate Veracruz and Chavín de Huantar.

RECITE/REVIEW

Multiple Choice

1. The environment of the New World hunter-gatherers would be transformed by
   a. retreat of the glaciers.
   b. large scale expansion of desert areas.
   c. decrease in diversified types of environmental areas.
   d. a cooler and drier climate.

2. Which one of the following is **NOT** true of early North Americans?
    a. They came in several waves of migration from Asia across the Bering Strait.
    b. They were ethnically related to the East Asian peoples.
    c. They were a uniformly primitive collection of tribes.
    d. They hunted to the point of overkill, leading to the extinction of many whole species.

3. Animists emphasize
    a. a creator God.
    b. not eating meat.
    c. harmony with nature.
    d. the divinity of animals.

4. Artistically Olmec heads are particularly noteworthy because
    a. they are larger than any other earlier sculpture including Egyptian.
    b. the motifs were so distinctly East Asian in origin.
    c. the bronze castings weigh at least fifteen tons.
    d. the carving is very realistic.

5. This creature or group of creatures is a common motif of both Olmec and Chavín peoples:
    a. megafauna, especially buffalo   c. birds, particularly condors and eagles
    b. felines, especially jaguar   d. snakes

6. Centers like La Venta and Chavín de Huantar were probably run by
    a. solders.   c. priests.
    b. peasant workers.   d. women.

7. A striking feature of Chavín agriculture was
    a. the large variety of corps.
    b. elaborate systems of terracing.
    c. the absence of it.
    d. lack of meat producing animals.

8. The name Olmec comes from the
    a. Incas.
    b. Aztecs.
    c. Spanish.
    d. Mayans.

9. While little is known about the spread of Chavín culture, one possible theory is that it was tied to
    a. new religious beliefs and improved foodstuffs.
    b. the rise of a centralized state.
    c. trade with the Olmecs.
    d. the rule of warrior priests in confederated provinces.

Short Essay

10. What is the commonality between magafauna, "Fulsome points", and buffalo?
11. What is the commonality between La Venta, Veracruz and Olmec heads?

Extended Essay

12. Describe the variety of environmental regions in North America and discuss the connection between environment and way of life.
13. Compare the Olmec and Chavín cultures.

Timeline and Maps

14. In terms of time, Chavín and Olmec were
    a. roughly contemporaneous.
    b. at least a millennium apart.
    c. developed in Central America at the same time.
    d. connected with Olmec growing out of Chavín.

15. Both Olmec and Chavín cultures developed by
    a. 2000 B.C.E.
    b. 900 B.C.E.
    c. 400 B.C.E.
    d. 25 B.C.E.

16. Which one of the following does **NOT** describe the location of the Olmecs?
    a. Caribbean side of Mexico
    b. Veracruz
    c. La Venta
    d. Chavín de Huantar

17. Which one of the following is **NOT** included in modern areas once Olmec?
    a. Mexico
    b. Panama
    c. Guatemala
    d. Honduras

18. Chavín culture covered
    a. almost all of Mesoamerica.
    b. Arizona, New Mexico, Colorado, Nevada and parts of California.
    c. Peru, Bolivia, Ecuador and northern Chile and Argentina.
    d. the Caribbean Islands.

ANSWERS

Multiple Choice:
1. a, p. 129
2. c, p. 129
3. c, p. 130
4. d, p. 132
5. b, p. 132
6. c, pp. 132, 134
7. b, p. 134
8. b, p. 131
9. a, p. 134

Short Essay:
10. p. 130
11. p. 132

Extended Essay:
12. total chapter
13. pp. 130-35

Timeline and Maps:
14. a, pp. 131, 133
15. c. pp. 131-133
16. d, p. 129
17. b, p. 131
18. c, p. 133

10

WHIRLWIND HAS UNSEATED ZEUS: CULTURAL EVOLUTION IN HISTORY

SURVEY

Chapter Overview: Two approaches to try and explain the existence of similarities and common patterns in the human venture are cultural diffusion and parallel development. Each explanation has examples, strengths and weaknesses but not absolute proof. Look at the chapter outline on p. 137 and read the chapter summary on p. 143.

Chapter Objectives: After reading this chapter and applying the study method given, you should be able to:

1. Explain the theory of cultural diffusion and the arguments that support it.
2. Explain the theory of parallel evolution and the arguments that support it.
3. Compare the theories of parallel diffusion and parallel evolution.
4. **Making Connections:** Evaluate the theories of cultural diffusion and parallel evolution by applying examples of materials you have learned from studying Chapters 1 to 9.

QUESTIONS/READ

DIFFUSION VERSUS PARALLEL EVOLUTION: How do cultures evolve through diffusion or parallel evolution? Why are these presented as opposing views?

Cultural Diffusion: What is cultural diffusion? What are some examples of diffusion of culture over parts of the world? What cannot or does not need to be explained by diffusion?

Parallel Evolution: What is the theory of evolution? What are some examples of parallel evolution? Who were the major trading peoples of early history and what effects does trade have on diffusion? What does the "possibility" of voyages prove? In the early years, what explanations must we accept for similarities between widely separated cultures?

PARALLEL DEVELOPMENTS AROUND THE GLOBE: What parallel developments are covered here? How does each of them illustrate issues of cultural diffusion versus independent development?

Agriculture in the Americas: What was the advantage of agricultural development? How does agriculture in the Americas illustrate the complexity of cultural diffusion versus independent evolution? Why do archaeologists argue that the two centers of agriculture in the Americas evolved independently?

Ironworking in Africa: How does ironworking in Africa illustrate the issues of parallel or independent development? What unsolved problem is there in the steps of cultural evolution? What theories are there about the spread of ironworking and what problems do they have?

The Axial Age Across Eurasia: What was the Axial Age? What thinkers and/or beliefs were involved? How do they compare in ideas and or methods?

SUMMARY: What are the major points in this chapter?

STUDY SKILLS EXERCISES

1. **Making Connections:** Review the chapters in this unit, Ancient Civilizations: The Further Reaches. Go back and review the chapters in the unit on Ancient Civilizations: The Continental Crossroads. What are the similarities in any or all of the civilizations discussed in the two units? What are the differences?

2. **Reflection:** Have either of the two theories on cultural diffusion or parallel development been proven? Does it have to be an either/or situation? What cases or examples can you think of from Chapters 1-9, that could be explained by blending both points of view? What else would you need to know as an historian or archaeologist to verify either of these theories?

3. **Vocabulary:** None in this chapter.

RECITE/REVIEW

Multiple Choice

1. The theory that major innovations in the human venture develop in one time and place and then spread is called
    a. cultural diffusion.
    b. parallel evolution.
    c. cultural exchange.
    d. diffusion evolution.

2. The fact that there are similar patterns or structures of megalithic stones set up in many parts of the prehistoric world proves
    a. a common origin for all of them.
    b. nothing definite about their origins.
    c. that visitors from outer space must have built them.
    d. the builders must have been connected.

3. Reconstructed voyages between widely separated continents have
    a. not been demonstrated
    b. refuted
    c. shown that it is possible
    d. not been successfully attempted

4. Boats, trade, slash and burn agriculture and emerging political hierarchy are examples of
    a. parallel evolution.
    b. Axial age developments.
    c. cultural regression.
    d. cultural diffusion.

5. Archeologists have found that the presence of corn in Mexico and Peru proves that
    a. world agriculture originated in Mexico.
    b. agriculture began in Peru and spread to Mexico.
    c. agriculture originated in the Near East and spread to the New World.
    d. Peru obtained corn but not agriculture from Mexico.

6. Ironworking in Africa
    a. spread from East Africa to West Africa.
    b. spread from Egypt.
    c. definitely proves parallel evolution.
    d. is still a disputed issue.

7. The Axial took place in
    a. prehistory.
    b. sixth to fourth centuries, B.C.E.
    c. 2000-1000 B.C.E.
    d. Neolithic times.

8. The period called the axial age was a major turning point in
    a. agricultural techniques.   c. art and architecture.
    b. science.   d. intellectual and spiritual searching.

Short Essay

9. How did humans understand the relation between natural and supernatural forces before the Axial Age?
10. Does cultural diffusion imply the superiority of the originating culture? Why or Why not?

Extended Essay

11. Briefly explain both the cultural diffusion and parallel development theories and summarize the explanatory strengths and weaknesses of both theories.
12. **Making Connections:** Discuss the possibility that both theories, cultural diffusion and parallel development, help us explain cultural evolution. Use specific examples from chapters 1-10.

ANSWERS

Multiple Choice:
1. a, p. 138
2. b, p. 138
3. c, p. 139
4. a, pp. 139-40
5. d, p. 140
6. d, pp. 140-141
7. b, p. 141
8. d, pp. 141-42

Short Essay:
9. p. 142
10. p. 138

Extended Essay:
11. total chapter
12. no change

OVERVIEW III

CLASSICAL CIVILIZATIONS (500 B.C.E.- C.E. 500)

This overview sets the stage for Chapters 11 through 17. Do not skip these overviews as they will help tie together the sections of the text and the book as a whole.

Questions:
1. What does the author mean by "classical civilizations"?
2. Why was "tone" important in identifying classic civilizations?
3. How did the classic civilizations of Rome, Persia, India, Han China, Axum, Mexico and Peru resemble their predecessors? How did they differ from them?

Map: Classical Civilizations, 500 B.C.E- C.E. 500, (p. 147).

COMPARISON CHART FOR OVERVIEW III:
CLASSICAL CIVILIZATIONS (500 B.C.E.- C.E. 500)
Photocopy this chart so you can use it for Chapters 11-17 (you need at least 5 copies)

THEMES AND PATTERNS OF CIVILIZATIONS	CIVILIZATION_____ (fill in name)
Geographic and/or historic setting (include major cities)	
Government(s) (include major leaders)	
Society (include class issue, roles of women)	
Economy (growth of trade-include major cities, goods and extent of trade)	
Science and Technology	
Literacy, writing, literature	
Arts	
Ideas and Values (include religion, philosophy, political ideals)	

TIMELINE: Photocopy this page as you will need at least one timeline for most of the chapters.

CHAPTER TITLE _____

|____|____|____|____|____|____|____|____|____|____|____|____|_

CHAPTER TITLE_____

|____|____|____|____|____|____|____|____|____|____|____|____|_

CHAPTER TITLE_____

|____|____|____|____|____|____|____|____|____|____|____|____|_

CHAPTER TITLE_____

|____|____|____|____|____|____|____|____|____|____|____|____|_

CHAPTER TITLE_____

|____|____|____|____|____|____|____|____|____|____|____|____|_

11

THE ETERNAL CITY: THE ROMAN EMPIRE (500 B.C.E.- C.E. 500)

SURVEY

Chapter Overview: Under both the Republic and the Empire, Rome built a major empire and left a major legacy both for themselves and the Greeks. Look at the outline on p. 148 and read the chapter summary on pp. 163-164.

Chapter Objectives: After reading the chapter and following the study method recommended, you should be able to:

1. Describe the beginnings of the Roman city-state.
2. Summarize the major features of the Roman Republic.
3. Trace the growth of the empire under both governmental periods, the Republic and the Empire.
4. Discuss the problems of holding the empire from Caesar Augustus to its fall.
5. Describe the various elements of Roman society and culture.
6. Describe the rise of Christianity.
7. **Making Connections:** Compare the Roman empire to the Athenian empire in terms of power and attitude that they were wiser and had the right to control others.

QUESTIONS/READ

THE ROMAN REPUBLIC: How did the republic develop and what were its major features?

The Roman City-State: When and where did the Roman city-state develop? How did the Romans compare to the Greeks? What was the status of women in the Republic? Identify: Greco-Roman, Etruscans, patricians, plebians, consuls, "struggle of the orders," tribunes.

Rome Rules the Mediterranean: How did Rome become involved in expansion and how great was their expansion in the Mediterranean? Who did they conquer? What was the structure of their rule of conquered areas? Identify: Charthage, Punic War, Hannibal, Zama.

The Roman Civil War: What caused the Roman civil war? How were class issues made worse by imperial expansion? What do Marius and Sulla symbolize? What was the outcome? Identify: proconsuls, latifundia, Graachus brothers, Cicero, Pompey, Julius Caesar.

Julius Caesar: Who was Julius Caesar and how did he build power? What areas did he add to his empire? What reforms did he undertake? Who were his rivals and why did the Senate fear him? What happened after his death? What period do we date from the reign of Caesar Augustus? Identify: First Trimvirate, Pompey, Octavian, Second Trimuvirate, Cleopatra, Antony, Actium. *organized by Pompey; included Julius Caesar.*

THE ROMAN EMPIRE: How as the Roman Empire established and organized? What was the time span of this second period of Roman history? What successes and problems were there in the Imperial government?

Augustus Caesar: What was Caesar's role in changing the Republic into the Prinicipate? What powers did Caesar hold? How did he restructure the government? How successful was he at holding power and why? Identify: Augustus, princeps.

The Roman Peace: What was the Roman peace? How was it achieved? What were the three particularly important material benefits of empire? What was involved in each? What the literal and practical meaning of Pax Romana? Identify: "good emperors," imperators.

The Crisis of the Third Century: What was the crisis of the third century? What caused the crisis? How was it solved under Dioclectian and Constantine?

Decline and Fall: What were the factors in the decline and fall of the empire? What was the role of the Germanic peoples? What are the differing views of historians on Rome's decline? What actually happened to the empire by the end of the fifth century? Identify: "barbarian."

ROMAN SOCIETY AND CULTURE: What was the role of Hellenic and Hellenistic Greece in Roman civilization? What things did Romans add?

Roman Women: What was the status of women in the Roman Republic? What are the characteristics of a Roman "matron"? Identify: *paterfamilias*, Julia Domna.

Art and Engineering: What were the major Roman achievements in art and engineering? How were they inspired by the Greeks? How did they go beyond them? What was the significance of Roman roads and aqueducts?

Poems and Plays: Virgil's Aeneid: How is Virgil's Aeneid an example of Roman ideals but with a connection to Greek legacy? How do the Romans compare to the Greeks in plays and poetry? What is the story of the Aeneid?

THE RISE OF CHRISTIANITY: How was Christianity shaped by Greek ideas and its development within the Roman Empire?

The Message of Jesus: What was the message of Jesus? How does his story connect to Roman history? Why was Jesus' message successful?

Christianity Under the Empire: What is the importance of St. Paul in the early diffusion of Christianity? How was Christianity similar to other eastern mystery cults? Identify: "sign of the fish", *logos*

Women in the Early Church: How did women aid in the rise and spread of Christianity? Identify: "house churches", Constantine.

The Triumph of the Church: How were Christians sometimes perceived by others? How did Christianity find social and political recognition? Identify: Edict of Milan, Theodosius.

SUMMARY: What are the major points of this chapter?

STUDY SKILLS EXERCISES

1. **Making Connections:** How did the message of Jesus connect to the ancient Hebrew religion and how was it later connected to the Greek tradition?

2. **Reflection:**
   a. The Romans are usually portrayed as pragmatic and conservative. To what extent do you think that is true?
   b. Heroes of the American Revolution such as George Washington are often compared to the Roman hero, Cincinnatus. What is the connection?
   c. Much attention is paid to the fall of the Roman Empire. On the other hand, why do you think it lasted as long as it did?

3. **Timeline:**

509 B.C.E.	traditional date of Roman Republic
285 B.C.E.	Romans conquer Italy and begin to expand empire
264-146 B.C.E.	Three Punic Wars (Battle of Zama, 202 B.C.E.)
133-31	Roman Civil War
31 B.C.E.-C.E. 14	Rule of Caesar Augustus and beginning of Roman Empire
31 B.C.E.-C.E. 180	Pax Romana
C.E. 313	Edict of Milan
C.E. 410 and 45	Rome sacked by Germanic groups

4. **Maps:**

a. **Classical Civilizations, 500 B.C.E.-C.E. 500:** p. 147. Make a map outline of the classic age and locate the Roman Empire. Continue to label your map as you follow these chapters. Compare the locations to those in the Ancient Civilizations maps on pp. 7 and 87.

b. **Growth of Roman Dominions Under the Empire, 44 B.C.E.-C.E. 180:** p. 155. Be able to locate Rome, Carthage, Byzantium, Palestine, Jerusalem, Wall of Hadrian, Wall of Antoninus, Gaul. Describe the general extent of the Roman Empire.

c. **Germanic Invasions of the Roman Empire, 4th and 5th Centuries C.E.:** p. 157. Who were the various Germanic groups that invaded the Roman Empire?

d. **Nomadic Invasions in Eurasia 4th and 5th Centuries C.E.:** p. 157. What group invaded both Europe and China beginning in the 4th century to 454?

RECITE/REVIEW

Multiple Choice

1. The Etruscans passed on the ability to read and write to the Romans but they had acquired it from the
   a. Greeks.
   b. Minoans.
   c. Carthaginians.
   d. Egyptians.

2. The patricians were to the upper classes as **THESE** were to the lower class:
   a. latifudia
   b. princeps
   c. consuls
   d. plebians

3. Rome's great rival in the Punic Wars was
   a. Minoan Crete.
   b. Carthage.
   c. Cleopatra's Egypt.
   d. Byzantium.

4. Imperial expansion brought the late Roman Republic
   a. land as far east as the Indus River.
   b. political stability and immense wealth.
   c. a long period of peace called the Pax Romana.
   d. economic, social and political unrest.

5. Hannibal was well-known as a great leader of the
   a. Germanic peoples.
   b. Egyptians.
   c. Carthaginians.
   d. Etruscans.

6. Marius and Sulla represent
   a. Rome's victorious leaders against the Carthaginians.
   b. military leaders who took over in the Roman Civil War.
   c. brothers who as tribunes of the people fought for reform.
   d. the other two partners in Julius Caesar's triumvirate.

7. Gaius Julius Caesar Octavianus held all of the following titles EXCEPT
   a. pontifex maximus
   b. princeps
   c. King of Rome
   d. Augustus

8. Which one of the following had the **LEAST** to do with the other three?
   a. "good emperors"   c. Marcus Aurelius
   b. Pax Romana   d. Edict of Milan

9. Which one of the following was **NOT** one of the actions taken by Constantine to halt the decline of the Empire?
   a. Christian influences.   c. barbarian invasions.
   b. internal weaknesses.   d. dividing of the empire.

10. The barbarian or preurban tribes most important to Rome were the
    a. Celts   c. Huns.
    b. Germans.   d. Slavs.

11. Most historians believe that the major reason for the fall of the Empire was
    a. Christian influences.   c. barbarian invasions.
    b. internal weaknesses.   d. dividing of the empire.

12. Roman women
    a. could legally inherit.   c. could vote in elections.
    b. were the head of the family. d. held no political power.

13. Homer is to the *Iliad* as this author is to the *Aeneid*:
    a. Horace   c. Cicero
    b. Virgil   d. Seneca

14. If you met under the sign of the fish in Roman times, it meant you were a
    a. Jewish radical pledged to overthrow the Romans.
    b. sailor in Roman navy.
    c. member of one of the mystery cults.
    d. Christian.

15. Which one of the following is **NOT** a reason why Paul is called the second founder of Christianity?
    a. He persuaded Constantine to legalize Christianity at Milan.
    b. He endlessly traveled spreading the message of Christ.
    c. He wrote many letters to Christian communities in the Mediterranean.
    d. His own conviction of the truth of the Christian message inspired others.

16. Women helped Christianity survive in the early period by all EXCEPT
    a. serving as deaconesses
    b. converting and baptizing others
    c. preaching
    d. avoiding martyrdom

Short Essay

17. Describe the major engineering feats of the Romans.
18. How could you best describe the relationship between Greek and Roman culture?
19. What are the main themes of Virgil's *Aeneid*?

Extended Essay

20. Your author calls the Romans "reluctant imperialists." Explain why many historians have concluded this. Include a discussion of how the Romans tried to govern their newly acquired laws under the Republic and then under the Empire.
21. The decline of Rome was not one spectacular event but a long and complex fall. Discuss both the long range and immediate reasons for the fall of the empire.
22. **Making Connections**: Describe the political order of the Roman Republic and compare it to the Athenian polis.

Timeline and Maps

23. The date 509 B.C.E. is significant as the
    a. traditional founding date of the Roman Republic.
    b. beginning of the three Punic Wars.
    c. foundation of the "good emperors."
    d. end of the Roman Civil War.

24. The three periods of the Punic Wars lasted from
    a. 264-146 B.C.E.
    b. 133-31 B.C.E.
    c. 31 B.C.E.-C.E. 14
    d. 31 B.C.E.-C.E. 180

25. Which one of the following describes the end of the Republic and the beginning of the formal Roman Empire
    a. 509 B.C.E.
    b. 285 B.C.E.
    c. 31 B.C.E.
    d. C.E. 180

26. Rome is located in
    a. Southern Italy
    b. Northern Gaul
    c. Central Italy
    d. Western Greece

27. The naval battle of Actium was fought between Octavia and Antony near the
    a. old city-state of Carthage.
    b. mouth of the Nile in Cleopatra's Egypt.
    c. island of Sicily.
    d. western coast of Greece.

28. This group launched nomadic invasions from China to Europe in the 4th and 5th centuries:
    a. Vandals
    b. Huns
    c. Slavs
    d. Goths

29. The Edict of Milan was promulgated in
    a. 285 B.C.E
    b. 180 C.E.
    c. 313 C.E.
    d. 313 B.C.E.

ANSWERS

Multiple choice:
1. a, p. 149
2. d, p. 149
3. b, p. 150
4. d, p. 150
5. c, p. 150
6. b, p. 152

7. c, p. 153
8. d, p. 154
9. a, p. 155
10. b, p. 156
11. b, p. 156
12. a, p. 158
13. b, p. 160
14. d, p. 161
15. a, p. 161
16. d, p. 163

Short Essay:
17. p. 158
18. pp. 158-60
19. p. 160

Extended Essay:
20. pp. 150-156
21. pp. 154-56
22. Chapters 9 and 11

Timeline and Maps:
23. a, p. 150
24. a, p. 150
25. c, p. 152
26. c, p. 155
27. d, p. 152
28. b, p. 157
29. c, p. 163

12

THE PILLARS OF PERSEPOLIS: PERSIA AND THE MIDDLE EAST (500 B.C.E-C.E. 650)

SURVEY

Chapter Overview: This chapter covers the rise and fall of the various Persian empires and focuses on Persian religion and culture. Look at the outline on p. 166. Read the Summary on p. 174.

Chapter Objectives: After reading this chapter you should be able to:

1. Describe how the Persians gained empire and maintained unity in it.
2. Discuss the differences between the rule of Cyrus and Darius.
3. Trace the rise and fall of the Achaemenids, the Seleucids, the Parthians, and the Sassanids.
4. Describe the faith of Zoroastrianism.
5. **Making Connections**: Compare the Persian Empire with the Roman empire.

QUESTIONS/READ

THE RISE OF PERSIAN POWER: Who were the Persians? How did they become masters of the Middle East?

The Middle East: What is the Middle East in terms of land areas? What is the topography of the area? How has climate affected it? What is the Near East? Identify: northern tier, southern tier, Thebes, Babylon, Persepolis, Damascus, Achaemenids.

Cyrus the Great: Who was Cyrus the Great and what characterizes his rule? Why was he able to conquer the New Babylonian Empire? Identify: Pasagardae, Croesus, Daruis I.

Darius the Great: What was the contribution of Darius to the Persian Empire? What was the political structure of the Persian empire? How did Daruis attain unity? Identify: Achaemenid, satrapy, Aramaic, Susa.

LATER PERSIAN DYNASTIES: What were the major contributions of the Seleucids, the Parthians, and the Sassanids? What became of each?

The Seleucids: Who were the Seleucids? What role did Alexander the Great play in establishing their rule? What did they contribute to the Persian Empire?

The Parthians: Where did the Parthians come from? What were the strengths and weaknesses of their rule?

The Sassanids: Who were the Sassanids and what were their contributions to the Persian Empire? What was the Sassanid system of power? What was the role of religion in the collapse of Sassanid rule? Identify: magi, grand vizer.

PERSIAN CULTURE: How did class and gender relations differ throughout the empire and over time? What was the role of Zoroastrianism in Persian life?

People, Classes and Genders: How did the population diversity influence government? What class divisons existed? How did gender relations differ throughout the empire?

The Faith of Zoroaster: Who was Zoroaster and what were the elements of his faith? What effects did the religion have on others? Identify: *Avesta,* Ahura Mazda, Ahriman, Mithra, Wholly Other, sacrifical fire.

The Art of Imperial Persia: What is the significance of the pillars of Persepolis? What do the ruins today tell us about the splendor of the city? What were the art motifs of the Persians? How did art glorify the Persian state?

SUMMARY: What are the main points of the chapter?

STUDY SKILLS EXERCISES

1. **Making Connections:** Compare the Persian empire with Qin China (Chapter 7).

2. **Reflection:** The author makes several comparisons between Zoroastrianism and Christianity. In what ways might the two religons be linked?

3. **Timeline:**

522-486 B.C.E.	Cyrus the Persian
500-300 B.C.E.	Achaemendis Rule
5th century B.C.E.	Darius I
323-250 B.C.E	Daruis and Xerxes fight Greeks
250 B.C.E. to C.E. 224	Seleucid Persia
C.E. 224-C.E. 68	Sassanid Persia

4. **Maps:**
   a. **Classical Civilizations, 500 B.C.E. - C.E. 500,** (p. 147) Locate the Persian Empire.
   b. If you are not familiar with the area, trace a modern world map and identify the following locations: Egypt, Afghanistan, Black Sea, Caspian Sea, Red Sea, Turkey, Iran, Palestine, Israel, Syria, Jordan, Lebanon.

RECITE/REVIEW

Multiple Choice

1. According to the author, the area from Egypt and Mesopotamia up through Palestine to Constantinople is
   a. the Near East
   b. the Orient
   c. Persia
   d. The Subcontinent

2. The Middle East stretches west to east from
   a. Morocco to Israel
   b. Libya to Syria
   c. Egypt to Greece
   d. Egypt to Afghanistan

3. When Cyrus began his quest for power, the overlords of the Persians were the
   a. Medes
   b. Babylonians
   c. Egyptians
   d. Assyrians

4. The significance of the conquest of Lydia was
   a. its central geographic location
   b. its abundant natural resources
   c. capturing the wealth of Croesus
   d. its enormous population provided soldiers

5. Cyrus conquered Babylon in
    a. 538 B.C.E.
    b. 539 B.C.E.
    c. 560 B.C.E.
    d. 529 B.C.E.

6. Satrapies were
    a. provincial governments
    b. royal governors
    c. bodyguards to the emporer
    d. satellite cultures around Persia

7. Darius brought unity to the empire through all but
    a. royal agents
    b. a single legal code
    c. uniform weights and measures
    d. concentrating political authority in the hands of the emperor

8. The rising power in the west that threatened the empire of Darius and Xerxes was
    a. Babylon
    b. Athens
    c. Mesopotamia
    d. Rome

9. The Achaemenid empire finally fell to the forces of
    a. Alexander the Great
    b. Julius Caesar
    c. Nebuchadnezzar
    d. Han China

10. The Hellenizing of Persia occurred during the rule of
    a. the Seleucids
    b. the Parthians
    c. the Sassanids
    d. the Achaemenids

11. The major contribution of the Parthians was
    a. reorganizing the empire
    b. conquering Rome
    c. linking East and West through trade
    d. implementing an official religion

12. Sassanid rule relied on barons and
    a. magi
    b. satraps
    c. pashas
    d. Zoroaster

13. The creator of all things, judge of all people and rewarder of virtue is
    a. Anahita
    b. Mithra
    c. Ahriman
    d. Ahura Mazda

Short Essay

14. What conditions allowed Cyrus to seize power?
15. How did common institutions unite Persia under Darius?
16. What were the attributes of Ahura Mazda and Ahriman?

Extended Essay

17. Compare the rule of Darius with that of the Sassanids.
18. What elements of Zoroastrianism were found in later Christian beliefs?
19. **Making Connections:** Compare Zoroastrianism with Hebrew beliefs.

Timeline and Maps

20. Cyrus established his rule in
    a. 550 B.C.E.
    b. 539 B.C.E.
    c. 331 B.C.E.
    d. 500 B.C.E.

21. The correct order of rulers is
    a. Sassanids, Achaemenids, Seleucids, Parthians
    b. Achaemenids, Seleucids, Parthians, Sassanids
    c. Achaemenids, Parthians, Seleucids, Sassanids
    d. Achaemenids, Sassanids, Parthians, Seleucids

ANSWERS

Multiple Choice
1. a, p. 167
2. d, p. 167
3. a, p. 167
4. c, p. 168
5. b, p; 168
6. a, p. 169
7. d, p. 169
8. b, p. 170
9. a, p. 170
10. a, p. 170
11. c, p. 170
12. a, p. 170
13. d, p. 172

Short Essay
14. pp. 167-68
15. p. 169
16. pp. 172-173

Extended Essay
17. pp. 168-70, 170-71
18. pp. 172-73
19. Chapters 4 and 12

Timeline and Maps
20. a, p. 167
21. b, p. 174

13

GOLDEN AGE ON THE GANGES: THE PEOPLES OF INDIA (200 B.C.E.- C.E. 550)

SURVEY

Chapter Overview: After the Mauryas, India was not politically unified until the reign of the Guptas. However, smaller prosperous kingdoms brought wealth and cultural achievements. See the chapter outline on p. 176. Read the chapter summary on p. 186.

Chapter Objectives: After reading this chapter you should be able to:

1. List the invaders of India, the path they followed and their impact on India.
2. Trace the emergence of southern India as a center of prosperity and power in this time period.
3. Explain the term "a nation of shopkeepers" in relation to India.
4. Describe the Guptas and the golden age they fostered.
5. Explain and compare how Buddhism and Hinduism continued to develop.
6. Summarize the basic artistic and literary achievements including their religious connections.
7. List the varius scientific achievements of the Indian people.
8. **Making Connections:** Compare this second golden age of India to the first one including religious changes.

QUESTIONS/READ

INDIA BETWEEN THE MAURYAS AND THE GUPTAS: What was he structure and unity of India during this period? What was the time period involved? What kingdoms did exist? How successful were they?

   Invaders of the Punjab: The Kushans: Where was the Punjab and who were the Kushans that invaded it? What was the extent of the Kushan empire? What two patterns characterized the invaders? What did some of the invaders add to Indian tradition?

   Kingdoms of the Deccan: The Tamils: What and where is the deccan and who were the Tamils who ruled it? What was the basis of Deccan prosperity? What effect did trade have on the Deccan ? Identify: Dravidians, Tamils, Pandyas, Sri Lanka.

   Nation of Shopkeepers: Why was India called "a nation of shopkeepers?" What materials and products were the basis of Indian commerce? What was the geographical extent of Indian trade?

THE GUPTA GOLDEN AGE: Who were the Guptas and what was their golden age? What were structures of their empire?

   Chandra Gupta I: The Raja of Rajas: Who was the second Chandra Gupta? What empire did he rule? Identify: Samudra Gupta, Chandra Gupta II,Kumara Devi, Magadha, maharajadhiraja.

   Samudra and Chandra Gupta II: What were the accomplishments of Samudra and Chandra Gupta II? What was the size of the Gupta Empire? Identify: Kalidasa, White Huns.

   Life in Gupta India: What was political and economic life in Gupta India? What were women's lives like? Identify: *sati*

ART AND INDIAN PIETY: What is the connection between Indian art and piety? What are the major examples?

Evolving Faiths: Mahayana Buddhism: What was Mahayana Buddhism and how did this represent a developing faith? What was the Hinayana branch? How does each view the Buddha? What are their similarities and differences?

The Hindu Renaissance: What were the major developments of the Hindu Renaissance? What was the status of religion under the Guptas? What kind of variety or religious expression became available? Identify: *Puranas,* Brahma-Vishnu-Shiva, lingam, bakhti.

The Art of Caves and Stupas: What were the elements of art centered in caves and stupas? What is the presence of Buddhism and the Buddha in the different styles of art? Identify: stupa, Sanchi, yakshis, Ajanta Caves.

Beast Fables and Courtly Love: What was the literature of beast fables and courtly love? Who was Kalidasa? Which religion inspired most of the literature of this period? Identify: Sanskrit, *Ramayana, Mahabharata, Panchatantra, Shakutala.*

Mathematics, Medicine and Science: What were the Indian accomplishments in mathematics, medicine and science? What is the significance of Arabic numerals? What western science affected the Indians? Identify: Nalanda.

SUMMARY: What are the main parts of this chapter?

STUDY SKILLS EXERCEISES

1. **Making Connections:** India was subjected to a series of invaders in its history. What was the cultural reaction of earlier Indian culture? Compare it to this period.

2. **Reflection:**
   a. Both Jesus and Buddha championed spiritual concerns, not material wealth yet the organizations based on their teachings became tremendously wealthy. Can spirituality and material concerns be reconciled or are they basically incompatible?

3. **Timeline:**

185 B.C.E.-C.E. 320	Indian between Mauryas and Guptas
C.E. 320-540	Reign of Gupta
C.E. 375-415	Golden Age under Chandra Gupta II
5th century C.E.	White Huns invade

4. **Maps:**
   a. **Classical Civilizations, 500 B.C.E.-C.E. 500:** (p. 147) Describe the extent of Gupta India. How does it compare to Maurya India in location?
   b. **Indian Empires through the Classic Age:** (p. 178) Be able to locate: Punjab, Kushan Empire, Kashmir, Andhras, Gupta Empire, Sanchi, Ajanta, Magadha, Bay of Bangal, Ceylon.

RECITE/REVIEW

Multiple Choice:

1. During the period 185 B.C.E. to C.E. 320, India could be described as
   a. basically unified under the Guptas.
   b. politically fragmented with various prosperous kingdoms.
   c. under the control of Persians in the North and Tamils in the South.
   d. relatively free of foreign invaders

2. Most invaders of India such as the Kushans came in by
    a. the Northwest frontier.
    b. sea from the Bay of Bengal.
    c. coastal attacks on each side of the subcontinent.
    d. Ceylon.

3. The Kushans patronized the religion of
    a. Hinayana Buddhism.
    b. Renaissance Hinduism.
    c. traditional Vedic India.
    d. Mahayana Buddhism.

4. Which one of the following is **NOT** a similarity between the Mauryan and Gupta dynasties?
    a. Tamils
    b. White Huns
    c. Dravidians
    d. Deccan

5. Which one of the following is **NOT** true of India as a "nation of shopkeepers?"
    a. They had extensive foreign trade from Mediterranean to China.
    b. Cotton, pearls, precious metals nad woods were major products.
    c. An elaborate guild system kept control of production and prices.
    d. Trade was concentrated in the North and did not expand to the arid South.

6. The term maharahadhiraja or great king of kings was claimed by the
    a. Guptas.
    b. White Huns.
    c. Magahdans.
    d. andhrans.

7. Which one of the following is **NOT** a similarity between Mauryan and gupta dynasties?
    a. Both began in the Ganges state of Hagadha.
    b. Both expanded west and south.
    c. Both had their glory days with the first three reigns.
    d. Both were equally well-centralized and intrusive rulers.

8. The most famous of the Guptas was not only a conqueror and diplomat but also a pattern of cultural life
    a. Chandra Gupta I
    b. Samudra Gupta
    c. Chandra Gupta II
    d. Kumara Devi Gupta

9. The decline of the Guptas was precipitated by
    a. a series of natural disasters.
    b. weaknesses in the feudal system.
    c. a decline in trade.
    d. invasion of the White Huns.

10. The Mahayana view of Buddha was as
    a. the greatest teacher that ever lived.
    b. an incarnation of God, a savior.
    c. a good model for monastic life.
    d. one of the many prophets but not divine.

11. Which one of the following was **NOT** part of the Hindu Renaissance?
    a. rise of popular worship such as bakhti, the lingam and lively festivals
    b. popularity of new religious literature such as the **Puranas**
    c. a trend toward monotheism
    d. tending to separate Brahma, Vishnu and Shiva

12. The main religious influence on sculpture and architecture in this period was from
    a. Buddhism.
    b. Islam.
    c. Hinduism.
    d. Greek mythology.

13. The best of Gupta painting is in these famous caves in the mountains of the Deccan:
    a. Sanchi
    b. Ajanta
    c. Karli
    d. Andhra

14. Which one of the following has the **LEAST** in common with the othe three?
    a. Kalidasa
    b. *Shakuntala*
    c. Sanskrit adaptation
    d. sati

15. Which one of the following was **NOT** an advance in Indian mathematics?
    a. Arabic numerals
    b. decimal system
    c. value of pi
    d. geometry

Short Essay

16. A current Sri Lankan rebel group calls itself the Tamil Tigers. What is the historical connection and significance of the "Tamil" part of the title?
17. What was the *Panchatantra?*
18. What were the varius effects the Greeks had on Indian culture?

Extended Essay

19. Illustrate, with specific examples, how Buddhism and Hinduism inspired Indian culture in the classic age.
20. Describe how India of this period fits the title, "a nation of shopkeepers."
21. **Making Connections:** Discuss how Buddhism and Hinduism evolved form the earlier Mauryans through the second golden age under the Guptas. Note likenesses and differences in their development.

Timeline and Maps

22. During this time period India did not enjoy unity, suffered foreign invasions and yet enjoyed great prosperity and kingdoms in southern Idnai:
    a. 185 B.C.E.-C.E. 320
    b. C.E. 320-540
    c. 2nd-6th centuries C.E.
    d. 31 B.D.-C.E. 180

23. The great reign of the Guptas was from
    a. 185 B.C.E.-C.E. 320
    b. C.E. 320-540
    c. 2nd-6th centuries C.E.
    d. 31 B.D.-C.E. 180

24. In terms of land, the Guptas, compared to the Mauryans, held
    a. more of the south.
    b. most of Ceylon and southeast Asia.
    c. only lands in central India.
    d. less of the south.

25. The headlands of the five rivers that flow to the Ganges is called
    a. Kashmir.
    b. Deccan.
    c. Punjab.
    d. Ajanta.

26. The Kishan Empire of India was concentrated in the
    a. Northwest.
    b. Southwest.
    c. south and central Deccan.
    d. Ganges River valley.

ANSWERS

Multiple Choice:
1. b, p. 177
2. a, p. 177
3. d, p. 177
4. b, pp. 178-79
5. d, p. 179
6. b, pp. 177, 180
7. d, p. 179
8. c. p. 180
9. d, p. 180
10. b, p. 182
11. d, p. 182
12. a, p 182
13. b, p. 184
14. d, pp. 180, 185
15. d, p. 186

Short Essay:
16. pp. 177-79
17. p. 185
18. pp. 183, 186

Extended Essay:
19. pp. 181-86
20. p. 179
21. Chapters 6 and 13

Timeline and Maps:
22. a, p. 177
23. b, p. 179
24. d, p. 179
25. c., p. 179
26. a, p. 177

14

THE GRANDEUR OF HAN CHINA: THE CHINESE EMPIRE (200 B.C.E.- C.E. 200)

SURVEY

Chapter Overview: The Han dynasty laid the foundations for imperial unity during their Classic Age empire. See the chapter outline on p. 188. Read the chapter summary on p. 199.

Chapter Objectives:

1. Summarize the growth and decline of the Han dynasty.
2. Outline the accomplishments of the major Han rulers.
3. Trace the growth of the Chinese empire and the foreign policies of Han China.
4. Describe the governmental, economic and social structures of the Han periods.
5. Discuss the impact of Confucianism and the survival of Legalism and Daoism.
6. Describe the cultural accomplishments of the Han.
7. Summarize the various forces of unity in China.
8. **Making Connections:** Compare the Chinese empire to earlier Chinese empires.

QUESTIONS/READ

THE HAN DYNASTY: When and where was the Han dynasty established? How did they come to power? How did they control their empire?

The Exalted Founder: Han Gaozu: Who was Han Gaozu and how did he found the Han dynasty? What type of person was he? What political course did he follow? Identify: Xiang Yu, Liu Bang, "people of Han."

The Sustainer: Empress Lu: Who was Empress Lu and why was she called the "sustainer?" How did she achieve this? Identify: Chang'an.

The Marital Emperor: Han Wudi: What did the "Martial Emperor" do to strengthen the empire? What policies did he follow externally and what areas did he conquer or ally with? What was the state of the Middle Kingdom by the time of his death?

Wang Mang and the Interrengnum: Who was Wang Mang and why is his rule described as an interregnum? What problems were there in the Han empire at this time? Identify: Former or Western Han, Later or Eastern Han, Red Eyebrows.

New Frontiers: Who were the Later Han and what new frontiers did they find? How did they restore and expand China? Identify: Xiongnu, Ban Chao, Silk Road.

The Mandate Passes: What difficulties caused the passing of the Mandate of Heaven? How was the Han Empire a victim of its own success? Identify: Yellow Turbans, Three Kingdoms.

THE STRUCTURE OF HAN CHINA: What was the governing structure of the Han empire? What was Han society like? What was the status of the economy?

The Imperial Mystique: What was the basis of Chinese imperial mystique?

The Scholar Bureaucrats: What was the scholar-bureaucrat system? What ideology was it based on? How was China structured and divided administratively? How did the Han develop this bureaucracy?

Sixty Million Chinese-and Counting: What was the population and size of China and how does it compare to the present? How does it compare to the U.S.? What things worked toward unity of this population? What was the basic social structure? How was the economy developed and expanded?

The Women of Han China: What was the status of women under the Han? What was the image of ideal womanhood in the Confucian tradition? Who was Pan Chao and what were her precepts?

THE MIND AND ART OF THE HAN: What were the intellectual and artistic accomplishments of the Han? What ideals were they based on?

The Triumph of Confucianism: How did Confucianism contribute to Chinese culture? In what ways did Legalism and Daoism survive? How was Confucianism transformed?

The Grand Historian: Who or what was the "Grand Historian?" What was the basis of Han historical scholarship? Who were Sima Qian and Ban Gu and what were their historical views and writing? What is the historical approach based on personality and the approach based on institutional analysis and impersonal forces?

Art in the Palace of Han: What are the subjects and styles of Han art? What aspects of Han art are seen in Gaozu's palace complex at Chang'an?

SUMMARY: What are the main points of this chapter?

STUDY SKILLS EXERCISES

1. **Making Connections:**
   a. The task of governing a huge empire was undertaken by both the Han empire and its contemporary, the Roman Empire. How do they compare? How does the reign of Han Wudi compare to that of Caesar Augustus?
   b. Compare the views of Chinese historians to those of Greek and Roman historians.

2. **Reflection:**
   a. Viewing history in a cyclical sense is a popular theory. What do you think is its appeal?
   b. Notice that Confucianism is distorted to fit the political and social views of the time. Why do you think this happens to the ideas of religious and philosophical leaders?

3. **Timeline:**

206 B.C.E.-C.E. 220	Han China
202 B.C.E.-C.E. 9	Former or Western Han
C.E. 9-25	Interregnum of Wang Mang
C.E. 25-220	Later or Eastern Han
C.E. 220	Three Kingdoms

4. **Maps:**
   a. **Classical Civilizations 500 B.C.E.- C.E. 500:** (p. 147) Compare the size of Han China to the dynasties of Ancient China.
   b. **Chinese Empires through the Classic Age:** (p. 190) Be able to locate: Chang'an, Loyand, Korea, Tarim Basin, Great Wall, directions of expansion of the Han.

RECITE/REVIEW

Multiple Choice

1. After the fall of the Qin dynasty, Chian experienced
    a. rapid political recovery.
    b. a long period of anarchy.
    c. lasting disunity till modern times.
    d. the period of the Three Kingdoms.

2. Which one of the following Han rulers is *not* correctly matched with a major achievement?
    a. Han Gaozu-founder of the Former or Western Han.
    b. Empress Lu-sustained Han power and the support of the people..
    c. Han Wudi-conqueror of the empire.
    d. Wang Mang-founder of the Later or Eastern Han.

3. One of Han Wudi's foreign policies established a traditional Chinese policy. This was
    a. expanding the Great Wall
    b. using barbarians to control barbarians.
    c. expanding the Mandate of Heaven to dynastic cycles.
    d. following traditional Confucianism.

4. Which one of the following has the **LEAST** in common with the others?
    a. Red Eyebrows   c. Yellow Turbans
    b. Daoist inspired peasants d. Confucian scholars

5. One of the most radical policies of Wang Mang was
    a. reestablishing feudalism.
    b. nationalizing noble estates and given them to peasants.
    c. overthrowing and permanently replacing the Confucian scholars.
    d. moving the Han capital from Chang'an to Loyang.

6. Unlike its Roman contemporary, Han China
    a. was efficiently centralized in its government..
    b. was often invaded by barbarian peoples.
    c. ruled a homogeneous peoples.
    d. moving the Han capital form Chang'an to Loyang.

7. As a way of keeping unity, the Han continued the policy of
    a. Legalism
    b. Daoist mystique
    c. Civil service exams
    d. Mandate of Heaven

8. Pan Chao was particularly noted for
    a. his expansion of China to the West
    b. her writings on Han women
    c. historiography
    d. novels covering peasants and commoners in Chinese society

9. Which one of the following is *not* true of Confucianism under the Han?
    a. It becomes an official government philosophy.
    b. It went beyond the original doctrines.
    c. It became scholarly and the basis for civil service.
    d. It was replaced by Daoism.

10. The model for Chinese history was the
   a. personalized history of Sima Quian's *Grand Historian*
   b. dynastic model of Ban Gu's *History of the Former Han*
   c. transformed Confucianism of the Exalted Founder
   d. Interregnum of the Wang Mang

11. The scale of Han public architecture can be seen in the
   a. Great Wall
   b. New capital at Loyang
   c. Silk Road
   d. Palace complex of Gaozu

Short Essay

12. What are the commonalities between the Red Eyebrows and the Yellow Turbans?
13. What were the major characteristics of Han art?
14. Describe the traditional Chinese dynastic interpretation of history.

Extended Essay

15. Trace the re-establishment of Chinese unity under the early Han rulers, Gaozu and Empress Lu.
16. Describe the society of China under the Han.
17. **Making Connections:** What traditional policies and characteristics from early China helped the Han maintain unity? Include a discussion of how earlier ideas were modified or transformed.

Timeline and Maps

18. The Former or Western Han dynasty ruled China from
   a. 206 B.C.E.-C.E. 220
   b. 206 B.C.E.-C.E. 9
   c. C.E. 9-25
   d. C.E. 25-220

19. The Han dynasty, both Former and Later, ended in C.E.
   a. 9
   b. 25
   c. 206
   d. 220

20. How did the China of the Han dynasty compare to the earlier Zhou and Qin empires?
   a. The Han was much larger
   b. The Han was concentrated in Northern China
   c. Earlier dynasties had more foreign territories.
   d. The Zhou and Qin empires were more connected with Rome.

21. Under Han Wudi, the Han Chinese extended west to
   a. Tibet
   b. The Indus River
   c. Tarim Basin
   d. Persia

22. The Han Empire took direct (not colonial) control of
   a. Vietnam
   b. Most of Korea
   c. Japan
   d. Taiwan

ANSWERS

Multiple Choice:
1. b, p. 189
2. d, p. 192
3. b, p. 191
4. d, pp. 192-93
5. b, p. 192
6. c, p. 194
7. d, p. 194
8. b, p. 197
9. d, pp. 196-97
10. b, p. 197
11. d, p. 199

Short Essay:
12. pp. 192-93
13. pp. 198-99
14. p. 197

Extended Essay:
15. pp. 189-91
16. pp. 194-96
17. Chapters 7 and 14

Timeline and Maps:
18. b. p. 192
19. d, p. 192
20. a, p. 190
21. c, p. 191
22. b, p. 191

15

THE OBELISKS OF AXUM: AFRICA FROM THE RED SEA TO THE SAHARA (600 B.C.E.- C.E. 600)

SURVEY

Chapter Overview: North Africa's development connected to Mediterranean cultures while the Kingdom of Axum prospered in East Africa. Look at the chapter outline on 201 and read the chapter summary on page 207.

Chapter Objectives: After reading this chapter and follow the study method, you should be able to:

1. Describe the ties between Africa and Mediterranean cultures.
2. Trace the rise and fall of the kingdom of Axum.
3. Summarize the major features of Axumite society and culture .
4. Illustrate what archaeological finds show about Africa south of the Sahara during the classic age.
5. Outline the variety of goods and trades in all of Africa in the classic age.
6. **Making Connections:** Trace past and present connections of Africa to the kingdom of Axum.

QUESTIONS/READ

AFRICA AND THE MEDITERRANEAN: What cultures flourished in various parts of Africa including the Mediterranean areas? What were their major features?

 Greek and Roman Africa: What areas of Africa were connected to the Greeks and Romans? How were they connected? Why did the Romans want North Africa? Identify: Ptolemies, Alexandria.

 Alexandria: Where was Alexandria and what was its significance? Why did many different scholars come to the city? How was its grandeur connected to ancient Egypt? Identify: Pharos.

AXUM: Where was the kingdom of Axum? What were its major features?

 Axum and the Red Sea: What is the connection between Axum and the Red Sea? What ancient culture preceded it? Who were the Axumite people? Identify: Ezana, Habashat.

 Axumite Society: How was Axumite society established? What was the role of Christianity in Axumite history? Identify: Adulis.

 The Culture of Axum: What were the elements of Axumite culture? What was the role of Christianity in Axumite history? Identify: obelisks, Ethiopians.

AFRICA SOUTH OF THE SAHARA: What were the features of African society south of the Sahara?

 Saharan and Sub-Saharan Cultures: What do we know about cultures in these areas in the classic age?

 Technology: Metals and Salt: What was the role of metals and salt in Africa's prosperity? What varieties of technology have been found? What is the significance of the Ghana "Axe factor" and the red jasper mine of Nigeria? Where was gold mining concentrated? Why was salt more crucial to settled society?

Trade-The Camel Revolution: What was the camel revolution and why was it significant to trade? What variety of goods were part of the trade? What African people adopted the camels and became the traders?

SUMMARY: What are the main points of this chapter?

STUDY SKILLS

1. **Making Connections:** Why would Alexandria have such a rich legacy from ancient Egyptians and the Hellenistic Greeks?

2. **Reflection:** How important is the role of geography in Africa's history?

3. **Timeline:**

3rd century B.C.E.	Height of Axumite power
1st mellennnium C.E.	Gold Mining and Salt Works

5. **Map:**
   a. **Classical Civilizations 500 B.C.E.-C.E. 500:** (p. 147) Locate Axum and compare it to the site on the Ancient Civilizations map on p. 87.
   b. Using the map you created for Chapter 8, add any of the following locations if they are unfamiliar to you: Yemen (Arabian Peninsula), Lake Tana, Ghana (note: Modern Ghana does not correspond to ancient Ghana in location), Nigeria, Senegal, Zaire, Zimbabwe, Zambia, Senegal River, Mali
   c. Look at the map of the Roman Empire in Chapter 11, p. 155 and locate the following: Alexandria, Mauritania.

RECITE/REVIEW

Multiple Choice

1. In the classic age most of North Africa was dominated by
   a. Greece.
   b. Ptolemaic Egypt.
   c. the Carthaginians.
   d. Rome.

2. If you were a scholar in the Mediterranean in the classic age, the most exciting open city to be in was
   a. Alexandria.
   b. Athens.
   c. Rome
   d. Constantinople.

3. The Ptolemaic rulers of Egypt were
   a. Berbers from North Africa.
   b. Greek successors to Alexander.
   c. Axumite invaders from the south.
   d. Carthaginian exiles from the Punic Wars.

4. The prosperity of Axum was based on
   a. gold mining.
   b. colonial expansion.
   c. trading.
   d. salt works.

5. The Axumites were a combination of
   a. Habashats and Kushites.
   b. Carthaginians and Ptolemiac Greeks.
   c. Berbers and Egyptians.
   d. Bantus and Khoi-san.

6. In architecture, Axum is known for its
   a. towering harbor lighthouses.
   b. metal-working buildings and factories.
   c. roads.
   d. "stepped walls" and giant obelisks.

7. Which one of the following was *not* an effect of Christianity on Axum?
   a. improved commercial ties with the Near East
   b. isolation from other African peoples
   c. spreading it to most of east and central Africa
   d. strengthened them to survive

8. Which one of the following was *not* a metal or mineral commonly worked or mined in Africa in the classic age?
   a. semi-precious stones   c. salt
   b. copper, iron and gold   d. bronze and silver

Short Essay

9. What was the "Camel Revolution?"
10. What archaeological evidence points toward complex political forms in classic age Africa?

Extended Essay

11. Discuss the commercial links between the Mediterranean cultures and Africa in the classic age.
12. Trace the rise of the Kingdom of Axum including its Ancient connections and present survival.

Timeline and Maps

13. Rome conquered North Africa including Egypt by:
    a 323 B.C   c. 31 B.C.E.
    b. 264 B.C.E.   d. C.E. 180.

14. The height of Axumite power extended from the 3rd century B.C.E. to
    a. 31 B.C.E.   c. C.E. 180.
    b. 1st century B.C.E.   d. 4th century C.E.

15. The great Mediterranean city of Alexandria was located near
    a. Carthage.   c. Ancient Troy.
    b. the Nile Delta.   d. Crete.

16. Axum succeeded the ancient kingdom of
    a. Kush.   c. Mali.
    b. Habashat.   d. Carthage.

17. The Kingdom of Axum was located in what is today
    a. Nigeria.   c. Tunisia.
    b. Mauritania.   d. Ethiopia.

ANSWERS

Multiple Choice:

1. d, p. 202
2, a, p. 202
3. b, p. 202

4. c, p. 205
5. a, pp. 204-05
6. d, p. 205
7. c, pp. 205-06
8. d, p. 206

Short Essay:

9. pp. 206-07
10. p. 205

Extended Essay:

11. pp. 202-206
12. pp. 203-206

Timeline and Maps:

13. c, p. 207
14. d, p. 206
15. b, p. 202
16. a, p. 203
17. d, p. 203

16

THE PYRAMIDS OF MEXICO AND PERU: THE AMERICAS FROM THE MOCHICA TO THE MAYA (200 B.C.E.- C.E. 900)

SURVEY

Chapter Overview: A variety of cultures developed in the Americas in the classic age. The most impressive was that of the Mayan. Look at the chapter outline of p. 209. Read the chapter summary on p. 218.

Chapter Objectives: After reading the chapter and following the study method, you should be able to:

1. Discuss the spread of agriculture across North America..
2. Describe the civilization of Mochica.
3. Summarize the major features of Mayan culture.
4. Explain the connections between the ancient and classical age in Mexico and Peru.
5. Compare North, South, and Middle America in the classic age.
6. **Making Connections:** Compare the city-states of the Mayans to those of Mesopotamia and Greece, politically and culturally.

QUESTIONS/READ

NORTH AMERICAN CULTURES: What different types of cultures developed in North America at this time? What were their major features?

The Desert Southwest: Mogolland Hohokam: Where did the Mogolland Hohokam people come from and where did they settle? What is their significance to agriculture?

The Eastern woodlands: Adena and Hopewell: What areas did the Adena and Hopewell populate? What type of agriculture did they have and why was it limited?

Society and Culture: What social and cultural developments are found in the Northern American peoples of the classic age? How extensive were their trading contacts? Identify: Great Serpent Mound

SOUTH AMERICAN SOCIETIES: What major South American societies were there and what were their basic elements?

Growing Populations: Which areas of the Americas had a larger and more developed population? What was the reason for this difference? What process of state formation took place in South, Middle and North America?

The Mochica Pottery Makers: Who were the Mochica and where did they develop? What is the significance of their pottery making? What was the structure of their state and society? What other types of art and architecture can be found? Identify: Huaca del Sol.

Peruvian Culture: Why are conclusions about Peruvian cultures hard to firm up? What types of archaeological evidence exists? What are the Nazca lines?

MIDDLE AMERICAN CIVILIZATION: What is the major civilization of Mesoamerica in the classic age? What are the characteristics of this Mayan culture?

The Pyramids of Teotihuacan: What is the significance of the pyramids of Teotihuacan? What and were is Teotihuacan? What can we speculate about the political, economic, social and artistic power of this people? What is the significance of the Pyramid of the Sun?

The Mayan City-States: Who were the Mayans? Where were the city-states? What was the basis of their economy? What type of city-state structure did they have?

The Minds of the Mayans: What can we tell about the values and activities of the Mayans? What was the Mayan theology like? What were their advances in science? What were Mayan glyphs?

SUMMARY: What are the major points of this chapter?

STUDY SKILLS EXERCISES

1.   a. **Making Connections:** What similarities do you see in the religious ideas of various Amerindians? differences?
b. If you have been filling out the Classic Civilizations Chart, determine the similarities in these civilizations that Esler calls the Classic Age. Compare it to your Ancient Civilizations Charts. Reread the Ancient Civilizations and Classic Age Overviews I, II, and III. Do you agree that there is enough distinctiveness to call it a classic age?

2. **Reflection:** How could humans have constructed the Nazca lines? Why do you think some people like to quickly resort to more outlandish theories like flying saucers and ancient astronauts?

3. **Timeline:**

1000 B.C.E.	Mogollan and Hohokam move to settled farming
ca. 1000 B.C.E.	Emergence of Adena Culture
1st century C.E.	Hopewell Culture emerges
C.E. 300-700	Mochica Culture
200 B.C.E.-C.E. 700	Teotihuacan
C.E. 300-900	Classic Mayan Civilization

4. **Maps:**
  a. **Classical Civilizations, 500 B.C.E.-C.E. 500:** (p. 147). Describe the locations of the Mayans and Mochicas. Compare them to the Ancient Civilizations map, p. 87.
  b. **American Empires and Zones of Culture:** p. 211. Where are the early centers of Amerindian civilization? Be able to locate: Teotihuacan Mayan Civilization, Moche.

RECITE/REVIEW

Multiple Choice

1. In the classic age, the most advanced Amerindian cultures based on farming were in
     a. South and Central America.
     b. Mexico.
     c. North America and the Caribbean.
     d. South America only.

2. This structure is the largest representational earthwork in the world:
     a. Pyramid of the Sun   c. Great Serpent Mound
     b. Nazca Line   d. Huaca del Sol

→ Beginnings of Christian / ~~Islam~~ Muslim conflicts.

Know about Richard Lionhearted & French King (Phillip Augustus).
    → Know general stories.
    → Know origins of it (Pope ~~called~~ for it in response to Byzantine cry for help.)
    → Not so much to free Jerusalem as to free Byzantine from Muslim influence

☆ Columbian Trade (possible ESSAY.)

✓ Islam = ulama (know.) (kind of like rabbis.)

✗ Writings of Aristotle, Socrates, Aristophanes, Plato, etc. held by Muslims.
   → 1st to form opinions.

Mongols → where they conquered.
   → left infrastructure alone (gov't, religion.)
   → In Russia:
      ✗ - middle-class really suffered.
         - tried to tamper w/ society.
         - pillaged society.
   → know divisions of mongols.
   → Never conquered Japan.
      → Protected by water. (Japan, Britain, United States.)

✓ Chronological Order of Incas, mayans, Aztecs, & Anasazi in N. America.
   → look at timeline at end of chapter.

✓✗ Know Charlemagne's empire & influences.

✗ Know Columbian Exchange: What they sent here, what they took back.

✓✗ Really Know Mongols & their influence:

✗ Charlemagne's Relation to Islam Empire.
   → Dad was Charles Martel. Halted them in Spain (prevented them from expanding.)

3. We are able to tell a great deal about the Mochica because of their:
   a. written histories.   c. religious mythology.
   (b.) elaborate pottery.   d. glyphs.

4. Which one of the following was **NOT** true of the Mochica?
   (a.) They had small loosely organized city-states.
   b. They had large priest and warrior classes.
   c. They had elaborate construction both in irrigation and pyramids.
   d. Their men and women were highly skilled artisans in textiles and ceramics.

5. Compared to Egypt, the pyramids of Mesoamerica, especially Teotihuacan were
   a. mostly earthenworks rather than stone.
   (b.) larger and more numerous.
   c. all dedicated to the sun.
   d. smaller in size and number.

6. The political organization of the Mayan civilization was the
   a. republic.   c. feudal monarchy.
   b. small village   (d.) city-state

7. In science, these people were more advanced in many areas than the Greeks or Romans:
   a. Teotihuacans   (c.) Mayans
   b. Mochicas   d. Hopewell

Short Essay

8. Why did North America have the least complex cultures in the classic age?
9. What is the commonality between the Great Serpent Mound and the Pyramid of the Sun?

Extended Essay

10. Compare the Mochicas and the Mayans as civilizations.
11. **Making Connections:** Discuss the cultural accomplishments of the Mayans and compare their cultural unity to their political unity.

Timeline and Maps

12. Mogollan, Hohokam and Adena cultures all began to emerge by
    (a.) 1000 B.C.E.   c. 1st century C.E.
    b. 500 B.C.E.   d. C.E. 300

13. BOTH the Mochica and Mayan civilizations date from
    a. 1000 B.C.E.   c. 1st century C.E.
    b. 500 B.C.E.   (d.) C.E. 300

14. Teotihuacan lasted from 200 B.C.E. to
    a. 150.   (c.) 700.
    b. 300.   d. 1000.

15. Teotihuacan was the center of an advanced culture in
    a. Peru.   c. Southwest desert of North America.
    b. Panama.   (d.) Mexico.

16. The classic age Mochica was built on the ancient
    a. Olmec.   (c.) Teotihuacan.
    (b.) Chavin.   d. La Venta.

17. The Maya were located in
   a. the upland plateaus of central Mexico.
   b. coastal lowlands of Peru.
   c. Gulf coast lowlands of Mexico.
   d. Pacific highlands of Central America.

ANSWERS

Multiple choice:
1. a, p. 212
2. c, p. 210
3. b, p. 212
4. a, pp. 212-14
5. b, p. 214
6. d, p. 215
7. c, p. 218

Short Essay:
8. p. 210
9. pp. 210, 214

Extended Essay:
10. 212-14, 215-18
11. pp. 215-18

Timeline and Maps:
12. a, p. 210
13. d, pp. 212, 215
14. c, p. 214
15. d, p. 214
16. b, p. 212
17. p. 215

17

THE LONG VOYAGERS: CULTURAL DIFFUSION IN HISTORY

SURVEY

Chapter Overview: Cultural diffusion increased through migration, trade and cultural contacts during the classic age. Look at the chapter outline on p. 220. Read the chapter summary on pp. 228-29.

Chapter Objectives: After reading this chapter and following the study method, you should be able to:

1. List the major forms and extent of cultural contact in the classic age.
2. Describe the Bantu migrations and their effects on Africa.
3. Describe the seaborne migrations and their effects on Africa.
4. Discuss the land and sea connections between Europe, Asia and Africa.
5. List the types of goods that were exchanged on these routes.
6. Discuss the extent of cultural contact in the Americas.
7. Describe the effects of the missionary impulse as a form of cultural diffusion in this period.
8. **Making Connections:** Compare the level and type of contact in the earlier ancient age to the classic age.

QUESTIONS/READ

CULTURAL CONTACT: How did this cultural contact occur? What cultures were involved? What was the extent and impact of this contact for each culture involved?

    Forms of Cultural Interaction: What were the various forms of cultural interaction?

    First Steps on a Long Road: What is the implication of this title, "first steps?"

MIGRATION: AN URGE TO MOVE ON: Why did people migrate? What were the major migrations? How were cultures affected?

    Forms of Cultural Interaction: How does parallel evolution indicate the isolation of human civilizations? How does it indicate the interconnectedness of humanity? What are the significance of migration, trade and culture?

    Whole Peoples on the March: Why did whole peoples begin to migrate? What was the impact of this migration from earliest to prehistoric peoples to the present? What were some of the meldings that occurred from both the dawn and classic ages?

    The Bantu Migrations: Who were the Bantu? What was the extent of their migration? Why were they successful? How did their lives change after making iron tools? What happened to the Pygmy and bushmanoid Khoisans? What was the nature of Bantu society? Identify: Nok.

    Seaborne Migrations Across the Pacific: What types of migration took place across the Pacific? Who were the people involved? How did they travel such long distances? Where did they settle? Idenitfy: Oceania, Melanesia, Micronesia, Polynesia.

TRADE: VOYAGING BY LAND AND SEA: What were the main trade routes and traders in the classic age?

The Horse-Trading Impulse: What was the Horse-trading impulse? What was the difference between trade in the dawn and the classic ages?

Caravans Across Eurasia: What was the major land route and what empires did it connect? Who were the middlemen? Identify: Tarim Basin, Pamir Knot, Samarkand.

Riding the Monsoon Winds to India: What type of travel did the monsoon winds allow? What peoples were connected and involved? What trade goods were the most popular? What good traveled which directions? Identify: Malabar coast.

CULTURAL DIFFUSION: THE OUTREACH OF IDEAS: What particular ideas were diffused from one region to another in the classic age? What geographic areas were involved?

Definitions of Culture: What are the various definitions of culture? What was a major form of cultural influence during the classic age?

The Missionary Impulse: What religions displayed missionary impulse and which ones did not? What major world religions experienced the greatest diffusion in the classic age? How and where did they diffuse? Identify: Ambrose, Augustine, Jerome.

SUMMARY: What were the main points of this chapter?

STUDY SKILLS

1. **Making Connections:**
   a. Compare what you know about migrations in the present to those that happened in the past. Are the reasons the same or not?
   b. Look at the origins and development of Christianity and Buddhism. See if you can determine why they were more missionary oriented than other religions.
   c. When contact occurs by war, do not automatically think the conquerors impose their culture and no diffusion happens from the conquered. What of the opposite can you think of from the dawn and classic ages?

2. **Reflections:** Imagine yourself as any one of the travelers (migrant, trader, missionary) and then as one of the people whose lives were affected by them. What problems would be involved? What pros and cons could there be in the effects of this travel and contact?

3. **Maps:**
   a. **Dispersal of Agriculture:** (p. 222) What were the major centers of independent and possible independent dispersal of agriculture? What origin center had the most variety of crops? What crops reached Africa from Asia? What domesticated bird spread north from Mexico? Which area has the earliest date of a "settled farming" way of life? Which area has the latest? Write a narrative that would summarize the map.
   b. **Eurasian Trade Routes:** (p. 226) Be able to follow these land and sea routes and tie them to the material presented in this chapter. What areas had the most crossing and meeting of trade routes (both land and sea)? What can you determine about its significance from this map?
   c. Find a map of the Pacific and familiarize yourself with the Oceania locations referred to in the text.

RECITE/REVIEW

Multiple Choice

1. The oldest form of contact between peoples was
   a. trade.   c. exploring.
   b. migration.   d. missionary impulse.

2. In the middle of the first millennium B.C, Negroid peoples were concentrated in the
    a. northern Mediterranean coastal area of Africa.
    b. highlands of Ethiopia and Kenya.
    c. Sudanic savanna just south of the Sahara.
    d. western end or bulge of Africa.

3. By C.E. 500, the people of this language group had migrated almost everywhere south of the Sahara:
    a. Khoisian   c. Habashats
    b. Nok   d. Bantus

4. The above migration (question 3) seems to have been successful because
    a. there were no other inhabitants in Africa south of the Sahara.
    b. they were working in iron.
    c. they had domesticated camels.
    d. of a trading alliance with the Kushites and Axumites.

5. The people of the classic age that remained the most homogeneous despite migrations were the
    a. Chinese.   c. Axumites.
    b. Indians.   d. Romans.

6. The continents of Asia, Europe and Africa during the classic age were
    a. commercially linked to the New World.
    b. almost totally isolated from each other.
    c. linked by long-distance trade routes.
    d. too warlike to exchange goods peacefully.

7. The most popular goods in the Eurasian trade were:
    a. basic commodities like grain and salt.
    b. luxury goods like silk and spices.
    c. jewels.
    d. salt.

8. In the classic age, the Americas were
    a. in commercial contact with Eurasia.
    b. following interregional trade routes.
    c. developing short-range trade.
    d. not very involved in trade.

9. The religions which spread the most rapidly during the late classic age were
    a. Christianity and Buddhism.
    b. Judaism and Islam.
    c. Hinduism and Buddhism.
    d. Confucianism and Zoroastrianism.

Short Essay

10. What is the connection between Melanesia, Micronesia and Polynesia and what was their significance in this classic age?
11. Identify the term Nok and explain its significance.
12. Describe the cultural achievements of the Pacific Islanders.

Extended Essay

13. Discuss the Bantu migration and its effect on Africa. Include a description of the type of cultures established throughout Africa.
14. **Making Connections:** Compare the level of cultural contact from the Ancient Civilizations to the classic age.

Timeline and Maps

15. The earliest independent origin of agriculture was in
    a. Southeast Asia.   c. Mesoamerica.
    b. Middle East.   d. China.

16. The overland and sea routes connected these two empires in C.E. 200
    a Rome and Han China.   c. Kushans and Axumites
    b. Michicas and Mayans.   d. Catrhaginians and Guptans.

17. If you traveled the Great Silk Road from Samarkand to its eastern end, you would arrive in
    a. Adulis, Axum.   c. Loyang, China.
    b. Constantinople, Roman Empire.   d. the Ganges River Valley, India.

18. The monsoon winds took you across this major sea route of the classic age:
    a. Caribbean Sea.   c. Mediterranean
    b. Oceania portion of the Pacific .   d. Indian Ocean.

19. The greatest intersecting Eurasian trade routes took place in
    a. Europe.   c. India and China.
    b. the Middle east and Central Asia.   d. North Africa and southeast Asia.

ANSWERS

Multiple choice:
1. b, p. 221
2. c, p. 223
3. d, pp. 221-223
4. b, p. 223
5. a, p. 221
6. c, p. 225
7. b, p. 226
8. c. p. 225
9. a, p. 227

Short Essay:
10. pp. 223-24
11. p. 223
12. pp. 223-24

Extended Essay:
13. pp. 221-23
14. total chapter

Timeline and Maps:
15. b. p. 220
16. a, p. 226
17. c, pp. 225-26
18. d, p. 225
19. b. pp. 225, 226

OVERVIEW IV

EXPANDING CULTURAL ZONES (500-1500)

This overview sets the stage for Chapters 18 through 25. Do not skip these overviews as they will help tie together the sections of the text and the book as a whole.

Questions:
1. What does the author mean by "cultural zones"?
2. What are satellite civilizations?
3. What role did religion play in creating cultural zones?
4. What role did conquest play in creating these zones?
5. What happened to the disparate zones as the year 1500 approached?

Map: **EXPANDING CULTURAL ZONES (500-1500), p. 233.**

COMPARISON CHART FOR OVERVIEW III:
EXPANDING CULTURAL ZONES (500-1500)
Photocopy this chart so you can use it for chapters 18-25 (you need at least 7 copies)

THEMES AND PATTERNS OF CIVILIZATIONS	CIVILIZATION_____ (fill in name)
Geographic and/or historic setting (include major cities)	
Government(s) (include major leaders)	
Society (include class issue, roles of women)	
Economy (growth of trade-include major cities, goods and extent of trade)	
Science and Technology	
Literacy, writing, literature	
Arts	
Ideas and Values (include religion, philosophy, political ideals)	

TIMELINE: Photocopy this page as you will need at least one timeline for most of the chapters.

CHAPTER TITLE _____

|____|____|____|____|____|____|____|____|____|____|____|____|_

CHAPTER TITLE _____

|____|____|____|____|____|____|____|____|____|____|____|____|_

CHAPTER TITLE _____

|____|____|____|____|____|____|____|____|____|____|____|____|_

CHAPTER TITLE _____

|____|____|____|____|____|____|____|____|____|____|____|____|_

CHAPTER TITLE _____

|____|____|____|____|____|____|____|____|____|____|____|____|_

18 _____

CATHEDERAL SPIRES: THE RISE OF CHRISTENDOM (500-1500)

SURVEY

Chapter Overview: The process of civilizing Europe begun by the Romans was continued by medieval Christianity. Look at the chapter outline on p. 234. Read the summary of the chapter on p. 253

Chapter Objectives: After reading the chapter and following the study method recommended, you should be able to:

1. Describe the political, economic and social context of the early Middle Ages.
2. Explain the functioning of the feudal and manorial systems that allowed survival in the European medieval period.
3. List the causes and summarize the results of the revival of the High Middle Ages.
4. Describe the development and political centers of Eastern European and compare it to Western Europe.
5. Discuss the role of both divisions of the Christian church in the Middle Ages.
6. Outline the events involved in the collapse of medieval society.
7. Describe the cultural achievements of medieval Christendom.
8. **Making Connections:** In Chapter 9 your author called Greece the "fountainhead of Western Culture." Describe examples of this legacy in the Middle Ages and include the pathways through which they occurred.

QUESTIONS/READ

THE EARLY MIDDLE AGES: What was the time span of the early Middle Ages? What were the major features of this age? Why is this period often labeled the "Dark ages?"

    The Reign of the Barbarians: Why was this early period described this way and who were the barbarians involved? What areas did they rule? What three waves of invasion were there? Why did they move into Europe? What type of transition was it from Roman to early Middle Ages? Identify: comitatus.

    Charlemagne's Empire: Who was Charlemagne and what was the extent of his empire? What was the Carolingian Renaissance? What happened to his empire after his death? Identify: counties, Carolingian minuscule.

    The Feudal Lords: What was the significance of the feudal lords? How did the feudal system operate? What were the advantages and drawbacks of this system? Identify: vassal, seigneur, fealty, fief.

    Serfs of the Manor: What was the significance of the serf and the manor? How did the feudal system operate? What were the advantages and drawbacks of this system? Identify: three field system.

    The Life of the Church: What did the church provide to the Middle Ages? What were the two Christian centers and what areas did they convert?

    Women in the Early Medieval Society: What was the role of women in early medieval life? What were the functions they had at various levels of society? Identify: "taking the veil," Hildegarde of Bingen.

THE HIGH MIDDLE AGES: What was the time span of the High Middle Ages? What were the major features of this period?

The Rebirth of Cities: What caused the rebirth of cities? What crucial agricultural innovations were made? What were the effects? What prompted the revival of trade? How did trading among cities function? What was the nature of the commercial revolution that took place? Identify: guilds.

The Feudal Monarchs: What development took place in the feudal monarchy? What two countries became the most centralized and which one the least under the monarch? What techniques did the English and French kings use to increase their power? Identify: William the Conqueror, Philip Augustus, Louis IX.

The Feudal Monarchies: What problems faced medieval rulers? What was the significance of royal law in consolidating the power of the English monarchs? How did Parliament evolve? How did France differ from England? What concessions did the French king make to other great landholders, the Church, and the nobility?

The Popes and the Power of the Keys: On what did the popes base their power? What was the "two sword" claim? How was the church able to have more influence than monarchs? Identify: Gregory VII.

Women in the Later Middle Ages: What was the status of women in the later Middle Ages? How did it compare to the Early Middle Ages? Why did this happen?

EASTERN EUROPE AND BEYOND: What areas were part of Eastern Europe? How did it differ from Western Europe? What were the features of their societies?

The Byzantine Empire: Where was the Byzantine Empire? How did it compare to the West? How did the Byzantines protect Europe? Identify: Justinian, Theodora, Justinian's Code, Hagia Sophia, autokrator, Constantinople.

From Kiev to Muscovy: What was the significance of these two cities in the history of Eastern Europe? What influences made Eastern Europe different from Western Europe? What was the connection between the Byzantine Empire and the culture of Russia? Identify: Slavs, Varangians, "third Rome."

The Crusades: Rehearsal for Empire: What were the Crusades? What were the causes of the Crusades? What effect did the Crusades have on expansion? Identify: First Empire.

THE END OF THE MIDDLE AGES: What caused the end of the Middle Ages? What was the "autumn of the Middle Ages"?

God's Heavy Flail-or a Time of Change: What changes occurred that must have made many Europeans think God was punishing them?

Schism and War: Where did schism occur and what was the outcome? What war was taking place and what was the outcome? Identify: Babylonian Captivity, Joan of Arc.

Plague and Depression: What plague occurred and what was the outcome? What caused the depression and what were its effects, both positive and negative?

MEDIEVAL CHRISTIAN CULTURE: What were the essential elements of Christian culture? Who were the major intellectual figures?

The Daughter of God: Who was the daughter of God and what does her life illustrate about medieval culture? In what political conflict did Joan play a role? What did she accomplish politically?

Faith and Fanaticism: What was the effect of faith and fanaticism? What was added to Jesus' simple message? What was the Inquisition?

History 201   Final → Review

Quite a bit out of Red books
   → little blue books.

14 & 15th Centuries in Europe
100 yr. War = British & French
   → Skirmishes; intervals of peace,
       but not settled peace.
Depression. (economic downturn.)
Black Death (impacts.)
   - pop. decrease   - ↑ wages
   - ↑ food - mouth ratio
   - helped economy (long-term)
   - immediate impact - devastating
       → farmers not farming
       → shops aren't open

Byzantine Empire:
- nowadays: Turkey
- had a little of expansionist mentality
    → Not compared to Islams or Romans.

Charlemagne: Holy Roman Emperor.
  → liked to keep "Roman" in their titles
  as long as they can because it
  gives them authority.
  → Holy = declared such by Pope on Christmas Day
A Empire = Europe, but not British Isles.

Fuedalisms:
lords, vassals, serfs, fiefs.

✓ <u>fief</u> = land
<u>serfs</u> = work land
<u>vassals</u> = over serfs
<u>lord</u> = over lords.

} KNOW
FUEDALISM!

✓ Charlemagne's Empire (Check out map.)

✓ 1st People to Invade Russia = <u>Vikings</u>

✓ 1000 AD = Economic Revival.
   <u>Causes:</u> 1) expansion & revival of <u>trade</u>.
              2) Population increase
              3) New agricultural technology
                 → irrigation & drainage.

✓ Expansion of Muslim Empire:
   → Where they expanded and when
        they got there.
   ✓ → Never reach the Orient.
   ✓ → Restorationist of Islam = Muhamm
           → Know his story: where he
             came from, what he did.
   → Population centers of Islam (originall
B   1) Mecca & 2) Medina
          has khabla
          → capitals moved to Damascus
             and Baghdad.
✓ → Split into 2 Sects:
        Shi'ites   Sunni
   ✓ → predessors of   → predecessor should
        muhammed   be Abu Bakhr.
        should have been   → majority.
        Ali

The Twelfth-Century Renaissance: What was the twelfth-century Renaissance? What did it produce and why is it called a Scholastic synthesis? How were the Moslems involved? Identify: Aristotle, Aquinas.

The Art of the Cathedrals: What cathedrals were the center of medieval art? What were the characteristics of the Gothic style?

Medieval Literature: Roland's Horn, Dante's Hell, and the Canturbury Pilgrims: How do Roland, Dante, and Canturbury pilgrims typify medieval literature? Identify: *Song of Roland, Divine Comedy,* Chaucer.

SUMMARY: What are the main points of this chapter?

STUDY SKILLS EXERCISES

1. **Making Connections:** Compare the European feudal system to others you have studied in earlier chapters. Under what connections would a feudal system work best?

2. **Reflections:**
   a. Historians have found that periods of extreme change such as the fourteenth century seem to produce a great deal of apocalyptic doomsday thought. Why do you think more people would be influenced toward this in moments of social upheaval?
   b. Consider the cultural diffusion implications of having a Germanic Frank being crowned "Augustus" by a Catholic pope.

3. **Timeline:**

5th-10th centuries	Early Middle (Dark) Ages
11th-13th centuries	High Middle Ages
6th-1453	Byzantine Empire
1095-1250s	Crusades
1348-1600s	Black Death

4 **Maps:**
   a. **Age of Expanding Zones of Culture 500-1500:** (p. 233) Describe the zone of Christian Europe. What other zones touched it?
   b. **Dark Age Invasions of the West:** (p. 236) What barbarian groups invaded Europe in the 9th and 10th centuries? Where did each group come from and what areas did they invade? What modern day areas did Charemagne's empire cover?
   c. If you are unfamiliar with the geography of Europe, trace a map and label the following: Scandinavian, Iberian, Italian and Greek peninsulas, British Isles, France, Switzerland, Low Countries, Germany, Austria, Baltic Sea, Balkans, Caspian Sea, Rhone, Rhine, Danube, Volga, Carpathians, Caucasus, Ukraine.
   d. **Decline of the Byzantine Empire:** (p. 246) What was the greatest extent of the Byzantine Empire under Justinian? What areas of Europe did the Byzantines affect culturally? Locate: Constantinople.
   e. **Expansionism of the Medieval West:** (p. 248) What areas were conquered or reconquered by Christendom? What were the major Crusader routes to the Holy Land?

RECITE/REVIEW

Multiple Choice

1. Compared with some of its neighbors, Europe in the Early Middle Ages was
   a. culturally ahead.   c. economically prosperous.
   b. highly centralized politically.   d. less developed.

2. Which one of the following was NOT part of the series of invaders of Europe in the Middle Ages?
   a. Vikings   c. Magyars
   b. Huns   d. less developed

3. Charlemagne accomplished all of the following except
   a. unification of much of Western Europe.
   b. a revival of learning and the arts.
   c. passing on the foundation of a lasting empire.
   d. coronation by the pope in thanks for his military help.

4. Feudalism combined military defense and obligation with
   a. religion.
   b. trade.
   c. land tenure.
   d. conquest.

5. The economy of the Dark Ages was centered on
   a. the manor.
   b. long-distance trade.
   c. the cities.
   d. merchant guilds.

6. Which one of the following was **NOT** a cause of economic revival starting in 1000?
   a. agricultural improvements.
   b. Muslim technology
   c. population growth.
   d. revival of trade.

7. Merchants and craftsmen operated within the
   a. manors.
   b. feudal system.
   c. guilds.
   d. joint-stock companies.

8. The European countries whose rulers best succeeded in centralizing political power were
   a. Germany and Austria.
   b. Spain and Italy.
   c. Sweden and Denmark.
   d. France and England.

9. In the "two swords" view, this body was custodian of both spiritual and secular power.
   a. Catholic Church
   b. Byzantine Patriarchy
   c. monarchy
   d. Estates General

10. Who was the captive in the "Babylonian Captivity" of the Middle Ages?
    a. Constantinople
    b. serfs on the manor
    c. Muscovite Russians
    d. Catholic Church

11. The first Russian state was ruled by the
    a. Byzantines.
    b. Mongols.
    c. Vikings.
    d. Normans.

12. Because of the Mongol conquest, the center of Russian political leadership shifted to
    a. Kiev.
    b. Moscow.
    c. Byzantanium.
    d. Samarkand.

13. Which one of the following was **NOT** one of the multiple catastrophes that occurred in the fourteenth and fifteenth centuries?
    a. Byzantine invasion
    b. Hundred Years War
    c. economic depression
    d. Black Death

14. The epic poem, *Song of Roland,* chronicles
    a. the heroics of the knights of the First Crusade.
    b. William the Conqueror's invasion of England.
    c. a mythic warrior of Charlemagne fighting the Muslims.
    d. the adventures of a great Viking warrior in Russia.

Short Essay

15. Explain the connection between vassals, seigneurs and fiefs.
16. How were William the Conqueror and Philip August alike in their pursuit of monarchial control and power?
17. Who was the "master of those who know" and how was this significant to medieval culture?
18. What synthesis were Thomas Aquinas and other medieval scholars trying to achieve?

Extended Essay

19. Describe the art of medieval cathedrals and evaluate the use of the cathedral as a symbol of the Middle Ages.
20. Compare the roles of women in early and high medieval society. Try to account for the difference.
21. **Making Connections:** Discuss, with specific examples, how the Greco-Roman heritage affected European culture.

Timeline and Maps

22. The early Middle or Dark Ages were from
    a. 5th-10th centuries.
    b. 11th-13th centuries.
    c. 1095-1250.
    d. 1348-1600s

23. The Crusades began in
    a. 800.
    b. 1066.
    c. 1095
    d. 1348.

24. The Byzantine Empire would fall to the Muslims in
    a. 800.
    b. 1066.
    c. 1348.
    d. 1453.

25. In location, the Byzantine Empire was basically the
    a. eastern division of the Roman Empire.
    b. lands of Eastern Europe.
    c. remnant of Charlemagne's empire.
    d. Holy Roman Empire.

26. The Northmen were invaders from
    a. Russia.
    b. the Scandinavian Peninsula.
    c. Germany.
    d. the British Isles.

27. The Magyars invaded this area in the Dark Ages:
    a. Spain
    b. Sicily
    c. Baltic
    d. Eastern Europe

28. Which one of the following was **NOT** included in whole or in part in Charlemagne's empire or as a tributary state?
    a. France
    b. Germany
    c. England
    d. Italy

29. Under Justinian, the Byzantine Empire included all of the following except
    a. Italy.
    b. Egypt.
    c. Greece.
    d. Russia.

30. The main external cultural influence on Kievan Russia was
    a. Mongol.
    b. Byzantine.
    c. Muslim.
    d. Germanic.

ANSWERS

Multiple Choice:
1. d, p. 235
2. b, p. 233
3. c, p. 235
4. c, p. 238
5. a, pp. 238-39
6. b, pp. 240-41
7. c, p. 241
8. d, p. 242
9. a, p. 243
10. d, p. 247
11. c, p. 245
12. b, pp. 245-46
13. a, pp. 247, 249
14. c, p. 252

Short Essay:
15. p. 238
16. pp. 241-42
17. p. 251
18. p. 251

Extended Essay:
19. p. 251
20. pp. 240, 243-44
21. total chapter

Timeline and Maps:
22. a, p. 235
23. c, p. 247
24. d. p, 244
25. a, p. 244
26. b, p. 236
27. d, p. 236
28. c, pp. 236-37
29. d, pp. 244-46
30. b, p. 245

19

DOMES AND MINARETS: THE RISE OF ISLAM (600-1300)

SURVEY

Chapter Overview: Under the leadership of Muhammad, the Arabs predominated in the early Muslim world in three centers: Mecca, Damascus and then Baghad. Look at the chapter outline on p. 255. Read the summary on pp. 267-69.

Chapter Objectives: After reading this chapter and following the study method, you should be able to:

1. Outline the life and teaching events of Muhammad the Prophet.
2. Summarize the basic teachings of Islam including the centrality of the book, the law and the community.
3. Trace the rise of Muslim Empire under its early leaders.
4. Describe the development of the Shiites and Sufis.
5. Discuss the best examples of Islamic art, literature, philosophy and science.
6. List the elements that gave unity to the Muslim zone.
7. **Making Connections:** Compare Harun al-Rashid and his kingdom to his contemporary in Europe: Charlemagne and the Kingdom of the Franks.

QUESTIONS/READ

THE PROPHET AND THE HOLY WAR: Who was the Prophet? What were his teachings? What was the idea of holy war?

Muhammad, the Messenger of God: Who was Muhammad and how did he come to believe he was God's messenger? What did Muhammad preach? Identify: Allah, Omar, Hijrah, Islam.

The Social Message of the Prophet: What was Muhammad's role as prophet? What was Islam as a religious, political and cultural phenomenon?

The Islamic World: What factors contributed to the unity of Islam? How is Islam more than a religion? What is the significance of the "human dominion"?

Jihad: The First Muslim Holy War: What was the concept of *jihad* and how did it fit into the culture? Besides religious fervor, why did the Arabs expand and what helped them succeed? What was the extent of this early empire? How were the Jews and Christians treated? Identify: caliph, Omar, Poitiers, Constantinople.

THE ARAB EMPIRE: What was the extent of the empire? What dynasties ruled it? What were the main characteristics?

The Caliphs: Successors to the Prophet: What caliphs and dynasties followed Muhammad? What type of power did the caliphs have? Identify: "rightly guided ones," *ulama*.

The Umayyads: Who were the Umayyads? How did they rule? How did Islam spread under their rule? Identify: Damascus.

The Abbasids: Who were the Abbasids? Who was Abu al-Abbas and what groups supported him? What would happen to the original Arab conquerors? What three trends would develop? Identify: Harun al-Rashid, *The Arabian Nights*, Baghdad, *qadi,* Persians, Turks.

The Splendors of Baghdad: What were the splendors of Baghdad? What is The Arabian Nights' Entertainment? What was the effect of the Arab peace? What was the city of Baghdad like?

THE FAITH AND ART OF ISLAM: What are the basic elements of faith and art in Islam? What various groups are there in the Islamic faith?

The Quran, the Law and the Five Pillars of Islam: What is the Quran? What is the role of the law in Islam? What are the Five Pillars of Islam? What is the difference between Muhammad and Jesus as a leader? Identify: Islam, Allah, qadis, ulama, Sunna.

The Sufi Tradition: Ecstasies and Trances: What was the Sufi tradition? What was the basis of the Shiite split? How were the Sufis significant to the spread of Islam?

Islamic Art: Mosques and Minarets: What were mosques and minarets and how were they significant to Islamic art? How did the doctrines of Islam affect its art? Identify: Alhambra.

Arab Literature: Poems and Tales: What are the basic characteristics of Arab literature?

Philosophy and Science: Knowledge Lights the Way to Heaven: How were philosophy and science the best examples of Arab learning? What did Arab philosophy draw on? How did they go beyond it? What were their accomplishments in science? Identify: Avicenna, Averroes.

SUMMARY: What are the main points of this chapter?

STUDY SKILLS EXERCISES

1. **Making Connections:** How did the position of caliph compare to that of pope? How did each position evolve in this period?

2. **Reflections:** Holy war is associated with Islam because of the jihad principle but weren't the Crusades also a holy war?

3 .**Timeline:**

570-632	Life of Muhammad
622	Hijrah
630	Muhammad Returns to Mecca
632-661	Rule of "Rightly Guided Ones"
750-1258	Abbasids
946-1258	Decline of Abbasids under Turks and Persians

5. **Maps:**
   a. **Age of Expanding Zones of Culture:** (p. 233) Locate the Islamic zone and describe its extent.
   b. **Muslim Expansion to 750:** (p. 258) What area did Muhammad unify? What area of Europe did Muslims conquer? Who stopped them at Tours? What empire blocked them from Europe in the East? Locate: Mecca, Medina, Damascus, Baghdad, Cordova, Tours.
   c. **Expansion of Islam to 1500:** (p. 261) Into what areas had Islam expanded by 1500?

RECITE/REVIEW

Multiple Choice

1. The turning point in Muhammad's life and Islamic success was the Hijrah which means
   a. the flight to Medina.
   b. triumphal return to Mecca.
   c. a revelation from the Angel Gabriel.
   d. completion of the Quran.

2. Early Islam was basically a/an
   a. political empire.
   b. religious community.
   c. unified federation of allied states.
   d. group of city-state republics.

3. The Battle of Tours or Portiers symbolizes the halting of Arab advance in
   a. Spain.
   b. Italy.
   c. Byzantium.
   d. France.

4. The spiritual and political leader of Islam was called
   a. ulama.
   b. qadi.
   c. caliph.
   d. vizier.

5. Muhammad based his religious mission on the claim that he was the
   a. incarnation of Allah.
   b. messenger of God.
   c. Son of God.
   d. angel of Allah.

6. Which one of the following is **NOT** a trend of political history under the Abbasids?
   a. centralization.
   b. secession.
   c. decline of Arab supremacy.
   d. feudalism.

7. These two people undermined Arab Abbasid rule:
   a. Egyptians and Greeks.
   b. Mongols and Byzantines.
   c. Turks and Persians.
   d. Moors and Berbers.

8. This group insisted that the true head of Islam was not the caliph but blood relatives or descendants of Muhammad:
   a. Shiites
   b. Sufis
   c. Viziers
   d. Rightly Guided Ones

9. Islamic law was formulated by the
   a. vizier.
   b. caliph.
   c. prophet.
   d. ulama.

10. The cathedral was to medieval European art as this was to Muslim art:
    a. minaret
    b. Kaaba
    c. arabesque
    d. mosque

11. While the Arabs developed it further, their learning in philosophy and science was inspired by this legacy:
    a. Persian
    b. Greeks
    c. Christian
    d. Romans

Short Essay

12. What were the Five Pillars of Islam?
13. What was the significance of the qadi?
14. Who were the Sufis and how were they significant to the spread of Islam?

Extended Essay

15. Summarize the basic teachings of Muhammad and show how they would encourage cultural unity.
16. Discuss the three ruling centers of Islam and the early Arab world: Medina, Damascus and Baghdad.
17. Explain how the faith of Islam and cultural accomplishments of the Arabs were interconnected.

Timeline and Maps

18. Which one of the following is in correct chronological order?
    a. Hijrah, Rightly-Guided Ones, Umayyads, and Abbasids
    b. Abbasieds, Umayyads, Rightly Guided Ones, Hijrah
    c. Umayyads, Abbasids, Hijrah, Rightly Guided Ones
    d. Rightly Guided Ones, Abbasids, Umayyads, Hijrah

19. The Hijrah (which is the year the Muslim year 1) took place in
    a. 622.   c. 661.
    b. 632.   d. 1258.

20. The center of early Islam went from Mecca and Medina to
    a. Constantinople and Samarkand.   c. Damascus and Baghdad.
    b. Tours and Portiers.   d. Cairo and Cordova.

21. Arab advance into Eastern Europe was blocked by the
    a. Russians.   c. Mongols.
    b. Persians.   d. Byzantines.

22. Which one of the following did **NOT** have a significant area of Muslim expansion by 1500?
    a. China   c. India
    b. Persia   d. Africa

ANSWERS

Multiple Choice:
1. a, p. 256
2. b, p. 257
3. d, p. 259
4. c, p. 259
5. b, p. 256
6. d, pp. 260-62
7. c, p. 262
8. a, p. 260
9. d, p. 260
10. d, p. 266
11. b, p. 267

Short Essay:
12. pp. 263-64
13. p. 263
14. pp. 264-65

Extended Essay:
15. pp. 257, 263-64
16. pp. 259-62
17. total chapter

Timeline and Maps:
18. a, p. 256-60
19. a, p. 256
20. c, pp. 260-62
21. d, p. 258
22. a, p. 261

MERCHANTS AND MISSIONARIES OF THE INDIES: INDIA AND SOUTHEAST ASIA (600-1500)

SURVEY

Chapter Overview: India's political history is fragmented in this period but the culture continues to flourish as well as spread its influence into Southeast Asia. Look at the chapter outline on p. 270. Read the summary on p. 279-80.

Chapter Objectives: After reading the chapter and following the study method, you should be able to:

1. Outline the major changes in northern and southern Indian political history 500-1000.
2. Discuss the major changes in northern and southern Indian political history from 500-1000.
3. Describe the developments in Indian art and architecture in this period.
4. Trace the growth of India's cultural zone in this time period.
5. Compare the cultures of Southeast Asia before and after the Indian cultural impact.
6. Summarize the factors that supported the overall unity and timelessness of India's culture.
7. **Making Connections:** Compare the growth of the Indian cultural zone to that of the Christian and Muslim cultures of Eurasia.

QUESTIONS/READ

INDIA BETWEEN THE GUPTAS AND THE MOGULS: What was the political and social structure of India during this period? What elements of unity and disunity were present?

Attempts at Unity: Harsha and the Delhi Sultanate: Who was Harsha and what did he do to attain unity? What was the Delhi sultanate and where was the their empire? Identify: New Delhi, Cholas.

Invasions and Divisions: What invasions were there and what divisive effect did it have on India? What two power struggles took place and what was the outcome of each?

Rajput and Dravidians, Caste and Sex: What did the Rajputs and Dravidians add to Indian unity? What underlying order and assimilation prevailed and continued during this period? How did India become a single zone of culture during this period? How were caste and sex roles affected? Identify: Kshatriyas, sudras, Rajputs.

RELIGION AND ART IN INDIA: What religious changes developed in this period and what effect did it have on the arts?

A Ferment of Religions: Hinduism and Buddhism: What was the ferment that developed in Hinduism and Buddhism?

The Spread of Islam: How did Islam spread into India? In what areas of India did Islam have its greatest impact? How did the upper classes compare to the masses on harmonizing Hinduism with Islam and how does this still affect India today?

The Age of Temple Builders: What were the most significant art forms of this age? What were the design principles of Indian temples? Idenitfy: mandala, shikara, Khajuraho, *Descent of the Ganges, Dance of Shiva.*

THE INDIAN ZONE: SOUTHEAST ASIA? How did Southeast Asia become part of the Indian zone?

A Pattern of Village Life: What was the pattern of Southeast Asian life? What was the status of women? Geographically what is Southeast Asia and when was that term first used? Identify: Dong-son culture.

Missionaries and Merchants: What cultural diffusion effects did India have on Southeast Asia? How did this take place? How did it compare to the effects of the Chinese? Identify: Borobudur.

Land of a Million Elephants: From Malacca to Angkor Wat: What is both the broad and specific meaning of the phrase: "land of a million elephants?" What was the basis of Malacca's power? What and where was the kingdom of Kambuja and how is it an example of the Indian cultural zone? Identify: Borbudur, Palambanana, Pagan, Lan Xang, Malacca, Khmer, Angkor What, Suryavarman II.

SUMMARY: What are the main points of the chapter?

STUDY SKILLS EXERCIES

1. **Making Connections:** Compare the kingdom of Harsha with that of Charlemagne.

2. **Reflections:** As you have read these chapters, you have encountered pyramids, cathedrals, mosques and temples. What kind of statement or purpose do you think is involved? What building or type of building would be a symbol of modern America?

3. **Timeline:**

607-647	Empire of King Harsha
9th-12th centuries	Hindu temples in Southeast Asia
1192-1398	Delhi Sultanate
1500	Portuguese take Malacca

4. **Maps:**
   a. **Age of Expanding Zones of Culture:** (p. 233) What area does the Indian zone of culture cover? What other two zones overlap India in the north? What is the cultural effect of that overlap?
   b. If you are unfamiliar with the Southeast Asian area, create a map and locate these places: Burma (Myanmar), Thailand, Cambodia (Kampuchea), Laos, Vietnam, Malay Peninsula, Singapore, Indonesia, Java, Sumatra.
   c. **India and Its Sphere of Influence:** (p. 272) Describe the extent of India's sphere of influence. What modern day nations are in this sphere?

RECITE/REVIEW

Multiple Choice

1. Which one of the following was **NOT** one of the many foreign invaders of India from 500-1000?
   - a. White Huns
   - b. Rajputs
   - c. Khmers
   - d. Turks

2. During the period from 500-1500, the political activity of India was
   - a. unified under one large state.
   - b. divided between northern and southern kingdoms.
   - c. total chaos without any states, large or small.
   - d. centered mostly on the western coast in trading communities.

3. Which one of the following has the **LEAST** to do with the others?
   a. Tamils
   b. Chola
   c. Dravidians
   d. Punjab

4. Of the various religions in India, which one became **LESS** practiced in India in this time period?
   a. Islam
   b. Jainism
   c. Buddhism
   d. Hinduism

5. Which one of the following describes the views of the Hindu teacher, Sankaracharya?
   a. a mystical union with the Absolute Soul of the universe
   b. consecrating the princes as devarajas or god-kings
   c. blending his faith with that of Buddhism and Islam
   d. celebrating the polytheism of the Hindu religion

6. The response of the Brahmans to foreign intruders was to
   a. declare holy war against all foreigners.
   b. ignore them and retreat to the Himalayas.
   c. condemn them as untouchables.
   d. fit them into the caste system.

7. Indian temples featured a shikara or tower representing
   a. the square and circular blend of the world.
   b. the mountain connecting heaven and earth.
   c. a mythical pyramid from which the Ganges descended.
   d. monotheism and polytheism coexisting.

8. The Delhi Sultanate introduced this religion to India:
   a. Islam
   b. Zoroastrianism
   c. Christianity
   d. Daoism

9. Southeast Asian rajas were often converted to
   a. Buddhism.
   b. Hinduism.
   c. Islam.
   d. animism.

10. This was a famous trade center of Southeast Asia:
    a. Pagan
    b. Angkor Wat
    c. Malacca
    d. Lan Xang

Short Essay

11. How did Charlemagne's and Harsha's empires resemble each other?
12. Why did Buddhism fail to continue as a separate religion in India during this time period?
13. How did the term Southeast Asia come into being and what areas are included in the definition?
14. What is the commonality between Kambuja, Khmer and Angkor Wat?

Extended Essay

15. Describe with specific illustrations the age of temple builders in India.
16. Summarize the pattern of Southeast Asian village life. Include effects on later societies.
17. **Making Connections:** Compare the Delhi sultante with Maurya and Gupta India.

Timeline and Maps

18. The reign of King Harsha was from
    - a. 607-647
    - b. 1001-1023
    - c. 1192-1222
    - d. 1472-155

19. The thirteenth to sixteenth centuries encompass the reign of the
    - a. Khmers of Kampuja.
    - b. Delhi Sultanate.
    - c. Burmese Pagan.
    - d. Lan Xang.

20. India's zone of culture mainly extended to
    - a. Mongolia.
    - b. east African coast.
    - c. Southeast Asia.
    - d. Persia.

21. The city of Angkor Thom and the temple complex of Angkor Wat are in what modern day Southeast Asian country?
    - a. Burma
    - b. Thailand
    - c. Indonesia
    - d. Cambodia

ANSWERS

Multiple Choice
1. c, p. 271
2. b, p. 271
3. d, p. 271
4. c, p. 274
5. a, p. 274
6. d, p. 272
7. b, p. 276
8. a, p. 275
9. b, p. 278
10. c, p. 278

Short Essay:
11. pp. 235-38, 271
12. pp. 274-75
13. p. 277
14. p. 278

Extended Essay:
15. pp. 275-77
16. p. 277
17. Chapters 6, 13, and 20.

Timeline and Maps:
18. a, p. 271
19. b, p. 271
20. c, p. 272
21. d, p. 278

21

THE FIRST MERITOCRACY: CHINA AND EAST ASIA (600-1250)

SURVEY

Chapter Overview: While China experienced disunity in this period it also saw the great dynasties of Tan and Song and an expanding zone of influence to Vietnam, Korea and Japan. Look at the chapter outline on p. 281. Read the summary on p. 296.

Chapter Objectives: After reading the chapter and following the study method, you should be able to:

1. Discuss the accomplishments of these Tang rulers: Tang Taizong, Wu Zeitian and Tang Xuanzong.
2. Summarize the political, economic and social features and accomplishments of the Tang and Song.
3. Describe the weaknesses and unsolved problems of the Tang and Song dynasties.
4. Explain the impact of Buddhism on China and the changes in Confuscianism.
5. List the variety and type of China's scientific and technological activity.
6. Summarize the characteristics of Tang and Song art and literature.
7. Describe China's sphere of influence and its successes and/or failures in each.
8. Compare Vietnam, Korea and Japan in their contact and cultural diffusion from China.
9. Summarize the main features of early Japanese civilization.
10. **Making Connections:** Illustrate how China of this period built on specific previous dynasties and compared to them in achievement.

QUESTIONS/READ

THE TANG DYNASTY: When did the Tang dynasty rule China? What were its major features?

   The Center of the World: Why could China justifiably see itself as the center of the world? How would a traditional Chinese see the "Pacific rim" publicity of today?

   The Six Dynasties: What type of period was the Six Dynasties politically? In what direction did Chinese culture move? What did the Sui dynasty accomplish? How were they like the Qin?

   The Founder of the Tang: Tang Taizong: Who was Tang Taizong and what made him the greatest of emperors? What governmental reforms did he establish? Identify: Li Shimin.

   The Greatest Empress: Wu Zetain: Who was Wu Zetain and what actions earned her the title of the greatest empress? How did she solve China's foreign policy problems?

   The Brilliant Emperor: Tang Xuanzong: Who was Tang Xuanzong? Why was he called the Brilliant Emperor? What happened when he tried to expand to the West in Central Asia? Identify: Talas River defeat.

   The World's Largest Country: What was the status of China? What was the capital of Chang'an like? How did the Confucian exam system work?

Equal Fields and Wide Empire: What was the "equal-field" system? What was the role of the Tang government in the economy? How extensive was the empire and the reach of foreign trade?

THE SONG DYNASTY: When was the Song period of rule? What were its major characteristics?

The Five Dynasties: What was the period of the Five Dynasties? What happened to end the political chaos of the period? Identify: Zhao Kuangin.

Northern Song, Southern Song: What was the period of the Five Dynasties? What improvements and reforms did they make? What were the major foreign problems under the Song? Identify: Hangzhou, Wang Anshi, Talas River.

The First Meritocracy: Why was the Chinese government called the first meritocracy? How did the exam system work? What class benefited the most?

Economic Growth—and Problems: What revolutions occurred in economics? What changes developed in population and status? What problems did Song China face in spite of its wealth and prosperity?

SOCIETY AND CULTURE UNDER THE TANG AND SONG: What were the major cultural achievements of the these dynastic periods? What previous elements of Chinese culture endured and what changes did they experience?

The Condition of Women: What disturbing trends were emerging in the Tang and Song eras? Identify: concubinage, "lily foot".

Missionary Buddhism and the New Confucianism: How did Buddhism come to China: What form was it and why did it have such appeal? What changes developed in Confucianism? Identify: Tiantai, Qingtu, Chan or Zen Buddhism, Zhu Xi.

Science and Technology: From Gunpowder to the Printing Press: What types of advances did the Chinese make in science and technology? What emphasis did they have in their development? What were the varieties of Chinese advances in all areas? Identify: acupuncture.

Poetry: Moon in the Water: What types of poetry were produced? Identify: Du Fu, Li Bo, Su Shi.

Art: Mountains in the Mist: What are the characteristics of art in this period? What art were the Song particularly noted for? How did Buddhism affect art? What were the characteristics of Tang architecture? Identify: calligraphy, ceramics, Guanyin, Longment, Cave temples, lohans, hua.

CHINA'S SPHERE OF INFLUENCE: What was China's sphere of influence? How was China's culture diffused? How was it accepted in Vietnam, Korea and Japan?

The Borderlands: What were the two regions of borderlands? What was China's experience in these borderlands?

Vietnam: The Lesser Dragon: What was the Chinese impact on Vietnam and why is Vietnam called the Lesser Dragon? Who is the Greater Dragon? What was the history of connection between the two? What are the two "rice bowls" of Vietnam?

Korea and the Chinese Cultural Hegemony: How did Korea react to Chinese cultural influence? What was their political relationship with various Chinese dynasties? Identify: Silla, Koryo.

Japan and the Chinese Model: How was Japan affected by Chinese civilization? Why was China's impact more limited in Japan than Korea? What was the Heian period of Japan and what were its characteristics? Identify: uji, Shinto, Prince Shotoku, Nara, Kyoto, shoen, Fujiwara.

The Culture of Court and Monastery: What were the characteristics of Japan's twin centers of culture? Identify: Zen, Lady Muraski, *Tale of Genji*, bushido.

SUMMARY: What are the main points of this chapter?

STUDY SKILLS EXERCISE

1. **Making Connections:** How did the feudalism of Japan compare to Europe's?

2. **Reflections:** The Tang and Song both faced problems even though they seemed to have many advantages and power. Do you think success could only be sustained to a certain point by any ruling group? Does China's cyclical view of dynasties have any validity to you? Your author suggests the norm for human affairs may be division and disorder, not unity and order.

3. **Timeline:**

220-618	Three Kingdoms-Six dynasties
618-907	Tang Dynasty
751	Talus River defeat
907-960	Five Dynasties
960-1127	Northern Song
1128-1279	Southern Song
Japan: 1-7th centuries	Uji base society
710-784	Nara Period
794-1156	Heian Period

4. **Maps:**

a. **Age of Expanding Zones of Culture:** (p. 233) Describe the extent of China under the Tang and Song as well as zones of influence.

b. **China and Zone of Influence in the Tang and Song Dynasties:** (p. 286) Be able to locate: Yangtze (Yangzi), Grand Canal, Hangzhou, Kyoto, Nara.

c. If you are unfamiliar with the areas mentioned in this chapter, make a map and label: Manchuria, Mongolia, Tibet, Korean Peninsula, Indochinese peninsula, Oxus River, Talas River, Caspian Sea, Ferghana, Red River, Mekong River, Hokkaido, Honshu, Kyushu, Shikoku.

RECITE/REVIEW

Multiple Choice

1. Over her neighbors on the Pacific rim, China exercised
   - a. very little influence.
   - b. no influence.
   - c. political but not cultural influence.
   - d. great influence in all areas.

2. Which one of these has the **LEAST** association with the others?
   - a. Six Dynasties
   - b. Yang Jian
   - c. Heian period
   - d. Sui Dynasty

3. There were many similarities between Tang and this earlier dynasty of China:
   - a. Han
   - b. Qin
   - c. Zhou
   - d. Shang

4. The Empress Lu is to the Han as this ruler is to the Tang:
   - a. Cixi
   - b. Li Shimin
   - c. Lady Murasaki
   - d. Wu Zeitan

5. Which one of the following was **NOT** an accomplishment of Tang Taizong?
   - a. He founded the Tang dynasty.
   - b. He reformed the governmental system.
   - c. He expanded the Confucian exam system.
   - d. He ignored foreign conquest in order to rebuild China.

6. Under the Tang, this system gave more land to peasants although its intent was to maximize taxes:
   a. "collective-guarantee"   c. equal-field
   b. corvee   d. "lily foot"

7. A crucial weakness of the Northern Song was
   a. de-emphasis on the military.   c. expanding to Persia.
   b. lack of an exam system.   d. stagnation of trade.

8. The period of Five Dynasties was a transition between the
   a. Northern and Southern Song.   c. Han and Tang.
   b. Tan and Song.   d. Three Kingdoms.

9. The class that was most likely to produce a Confucian scholar-administrator was the
   a. warrior class.   c. aristocracy.
   b. urban dwellers.   d. gentry.

10. During the Song period the center of Chinese population and wealth shifted to
    a. the Northeastern heartland.   c. the eastern coast.
    b. central and south China.   d. western China.

11. The ordinary Chinese was most likely to follow this form of Buddhism:
    a. NeoBuddhism   c. Qingtu
    b. Tiantai   d. Chan

12. Thomas Aquinas was to medieval European philosophy as this thinker was to medieval Chinese Confucian revival:
    a. Zhu Xi   c. Want Anshi
    b. Zhao Kuangyin   d. Prince Shotoku

13. Which one of the following was **NOT** an invention of the Chinese?
    a. abacus   c. compass
    b. gunpowder   d. movable type

14. Lohans, Guanyin and Longmen cave temples point out the artistic inspiration from
    a. Islam   c. Buddhism.
    b. Hinduism.   d. Confucianism.

15. This area experienced overlapping Chinese and Indian influence:
    a. Korea   c. Japan
    b. Vietnam   d. Philippines

16. Early Japan was based on a simple society of clans or
    a. Zen.   c. shoen.
    b. Shinto.   d. uji.

Short Essay

17. What were concubinage and "lily foot" under the Song and what indicate about the status of women?
18. What did Du Fu, Li Bo and Su Shi have in common?
19. Who are the Greater and Lesser Dragons and what is the significance of the titles?

Extended Essay

20. Describe the meritocracy of China and discuss the value of such a system.

21. Explain how China had a long history as a Pacific rim leader.
22. Describe the impact of China on Japan but also include a description of Japan's cultural independence.
23. **Making Connections:** Compare the Tang Dynasty to the Han.

Timeline and Maps

24. Which one of the following is the correct order of Chinese kingdoms?
     a. Tang, Three Kingdoms, Northern Song, Southern Song
     b. Three Kingdoms, Tang, Northern Song, Southern Song
     c. Northern Song, Southern Song, Tang, Three Kingdoms
     d. Southern Song, Northern song, Three Kingdoms, Tang

25. The Heian period in Japan dates from
     a. 220-618
     b. 618-907
     c. 710-784
     d. 800-1200

26. Which one of the following was **NOT** in China's zone of influence?
     a. Korea
     b. Manchuria
     c. Vietnam
     d. Thailand

27. Nara is an ancient site in
     a. Japan.
     b. Korea.
     c. Vietnam.
     d. Central Asia.

ANSWERS

Multiple Choice:
1. d, p. 282
2. c, p. 282
3. a, p. 283
4. d, p. 284
5. d, pp. 283-84
6. c, p. 285
7. a, p. 287
8. b, p. 286
9. d, p. 288
10. b, p. 289
11. c, p. 290
12. a, p. 290
13. d, p. 291
14. c, p. 292
15. b, p. 293
16. d, p. 294

Short Essay:
17. pp. 287-89
18. pp. 291-92
19. p. 293

Extended Essay:
20. pp. 287-89
21. total chapter
22. pp. 294-96
23. Chapters 14 and 21

Timeline and Maps:
24. b. pp. 282-87
25. d, p. 295
26. d, p. 286
27. a, p. 286

22

LORDS OF THE EURASIAN HEARTLAND: MONGOL RULE FROM RUSSIA TO CHINA (1200-1400)

SURVEY

Chapter Overview: Under Genghis Khan, the Mongols built the largest of the historic Eurasian empires. Look at the chapter outline on p. 298. Read the summary on p. 308.

Chapter Objectives: After reading this chapter and following the study method, you should be able to:
1. Describe the life of the nomads of the steppes.
2. Explain why the Mongols were too powerful and include a discussion of the leadership of Genghis Khan.
3. Describe what the extent of the Mongol Empire was and how it was governed.
4. List the reasons why the empire declined.
5. Summarize the experience of Russia under the Golden Horde.
6. Describe China under the Khans.
7. **Making Connections:** Compare the empire building of Genghis Khan to that of Alexander the Great and to other empire builders.

QUESTIONS/READ

THE NOMADS OF EURASIA: Who were the nomads of Eurasia? How were they able to create such a large empire?

Herders of the Steppes: What was the way of life of nomads of the steppes? What was their technology? Why did they have militarist tradition? What were their three patterns of migration?

Steppe Nomads and Civilizations: What types of contacts did nomads have with civilization? What was usually the result? Why were the nomads a potent threat and a formidable opponent? Identify: steppe gradient.

THE RISE AND FALL OF THE MONGOLS: What caused both the rise and fall of the Mongols? What cultural impact did they have?

Genghis Khan: Lord of all Men: Who was Genghis Khan and why was he more successful than other nomadic chieftains? What were his motives? What does his title mean? Identify: Temujin, Eternal Sky, compound bow, Kerulen River.

The Mongol Conquests: What areas were the targets of Mongol conquests? What areas did they actually take? What did Genghis Khan pass on to his successors? What were his military abilities? Identify: Kublai Khan.

The Mongol Empire: What was the size of the empire? How was it governed? What was the source of Mongol strength? What does Marco Polo's trip illustrate about the Mongol empire? Identify: Kakaorum, Great Khan, Jagati Khanate, Ilkhanate, Golden Horde.

The End of the Mongol Adventure: Why did the empire decline? What groups managed to beat them back?

THE IMPACT OF THE MONGOL IMPERIUM: What was the long-term impact of the Mongol Empire in its zone of influence?

Mongol Culture: What was the level of Mongol culture and what effect did it have? How was the culture affected others?

Russia and the Golden Horde: How did the Golden Horde rule Russia? What mark did the Mongols leave on Russia? Identify; Kiev, Tartar Yoke, Moscow.

China and the Mongol Khans: What was the experience of China under the Mongols? What dynasty did they verthrow? Which one did they establish? Who was the Kublai Khan and what were his effects on Chinese government? Identify: Cambulac.

Fall of the Mongols: What led to the decline of the Mongols? What was the Chinese attitude toward the Mongols? What Chinese dynasty drove out the Mongols? How did the Mongol experience affect China?

SUMMARY: What are the main points of the chapter?

STUDY SKILLS EXERCISES

1. **Making Connections:** How did the travels of Marco Polo illustrate the revival of the earlier trade routes of the classic age?

2. **Reflections:** Try to imagine the extent of Marco Polo's travels. Follow his route by looking at the Eurasian trade route map on p. 226 and comparing it to the Khanate locations on p. 303.

3. **Timeline:**

1206	Genghis Khan crowned
1240	Mongols take Russia
1258	Mongols take Baghdad
1260-1368	Mongols control China-Yuan Dynasty
1480	Russians defeat Golden Horde

4. **Maps:**
   a. **Age of Expanding Zones of Culture:** (p. 233) Describe the extent of the Mongol zone. What other zones did it touch and take control of?
   b. **Mongol Empire at the death of Kublai Khan:** (p. 303) What and where were the four Khanates? Locate: Karakorum, Kiev, Sarai.

RECITE/REVIEW

Multiple Choice

1. Steppe nomads followed three patterns of migration. Which one of the following is **NOT** one of them?
   a. a primary pilgrimage back and forth across a predefined territory.
   b. retreating from invaders and finding new territory through migration
   c. drives southward to look for city-based civilizations
   d. aimless wandering to find new hunting grounds

2. The key factory in the maintenance of the Mongol rule was
   a. a unique administrative system.
   b. the army.
   c. the division of the empire into khanates.
   d. traditional clan loyalties.

3. Mongol religion
   a. was based on Buddhism
   b. was monotheistic
   c. had little effect on conquered peoples
   d. was similar to Christianity

4. Which one of the following areas was **NOT** overrun by the Mongols?
   a. Japan
   b. Russia
   c. China
   d. the Middle East

5. The effect of Mongol rule on Eurasian trade was
   a. destructive because it closed ancient routes.
   b. minimal because of new sea routes.
   c. to shift it to the Atlantic coast.
   d. beneficial in reopening routes.

6. For two and one half centuries from the 1200s to the 1400s, European Russia was occupied by the
   a. Ilkanate.
   b. Golden Horde.
   c. Jagatai Khanate.
   d. Kublai Khan.

7. One of the effects of Mongol rule on Russia was a dampening effect on developing
   a. a strong army.
   b. authoritarian rule.
   c. a middle class.
   d. their own culture.

8. In China, Mongol rule
   a. promoted local political autonomy.
   b. stifled economic development.
   c. destroyed cultural life.
   d. strengthened central government.

9. The Mongols were finally overthrown by a rebel leader who established which dynasty?
   a. Qin
   b. Manchu
   c. Tang
   d. Ming

Short Essay

10. What was the government of the Mongol Empire based on? already existing beaurocracies.
11. In what sense did the Mongols help Moscow become a center of Russia instead of the earlier capital of Kiev?
12. Generally, how did the Chinese economy fare under the Yuan Mongol rulers?
13. What is the significance of Cambaluc?

Extended Essay

14. Describe Genghis Khan's rise to power. Include his own abilities and the advantages possessed by the Mongols as a group in building an empire.
15. Describe and evaluate the impact of Mongol rule on Russia.
16. **Making Connections:** Compare the cultural effects of the Mongol Empire to those of the Roman Empire.

Timeline and Maps

17. Genghis Khan was chosen as the great Khan in
   a. 1206.
   b. 1260.
   c. 1306.
   d. 1480.

18. The largest of the khanates was
   a. Khanate of Kipchak
   b. Khanate of Persia
   c. Khanate of Jaghadai
   d. Kahanate of the Great Khan

19. The Mongol dynasty of China, the Yuan, ruled from
   a. 1206-1260.
   b. 1240-1480.
   c. 1260-1368.
   d. 1368-1480.

20. The Mongol invasion of Russia weakened the traditional center of Russia at
   a. Kieve.
   b. Varingia.
   c. Moscow.
   d. Vladimir.

21. The Mongol capital of the Golden Horde was
   a. Kiev.
   b. Saraiu.
   c. Karakorum.
   d. Kerulen.

22. The capital of the four khanates was
   a. Kerulen.
   b. Cambulac.
   c. Samarkand.
   d. Karakorum.

ANSWERS

Multiple Choice:
1. d, p. 300
2. b, p. 304
3. c, p. 305
4. a, pp. 302-04
5. d, p. 304
6. b, p. 303
7. c, p. 303
8. d, p. 307
9. d, p. 308

Short Essay:
10. pp. 302-04
11. p. 305
12. pp. 306-07
13. pp. 306-07

Extended Essay:
14. pp. 300-02
15. pp. 302, 305-06
16. Chapters 11 and 22

Timeline and Maps:
17. a, p. 302
18. d, p. 303
19. c, p. 306
20. a, p. 302
21. b, p. 303
22. d, p. 303

23

KINGS OF INNER AFRICA: FROM GHANA TO ETHIOPIA (600-1450)

SURVEY

Chapter Overview: New zones of urban cultures developed in Western Sudan and earlier locations continued to produce new empires. See the chapter outline on p. 310. Read the chapter summary on pp. 319-20.

Chapter Objectives: After reading the chapter and following the study method, you should be able to:

1. List the major empires of West Africa and their distinctive features.
2. List the major empires of East Africa and their distinctive features.
3. Discuss the factors that led to the emergence of both the West and East African states.
4. Compare the process of growth in West and East Africa.
5. Describe the artistic accomplishments of West and East.
6. Describe the vitality of trade and life in the cities of medieval West and East Africa.
7. **Making Connections:** Examine the role of cultural diffusion through religion and trade in the cultures of medieval West and East Africa.

QUESTIONS/READ

WEST AFRICAN EMPIRES: Where were these empires located? What caused their rise? What were their major features?

The *Bilad al Sudan*: What and where was the Bilad al Sudan? What features contributed to the emergence of West African civilization? How were these nations governed?

Ghana: The Land of Gold: Where was Ghana and why was it called the land of gold? How was Ghana governed? What was its basis of prosperity? What trading goods did the Tuareg camel caravans bring and take out? Identify: Mande, Soninke, Mandinke, Almoravids.

Mali: Where the King Dwells: Who built the empire of Mali? How did the kings revitalize the empire and trade? What was Mansa Musa and what were his accomplishments? How did Arab traveler Ibn Batuta describe Mali? In what way was religion a divisive factor? Identify: Timbuktu.

Mansa Musa's Pilgrimage: What was Mansa Musa's pilgrimage and why did he take it? What cultural contacts took place?

CITIES AND KINGDOMS OF EAST AFRICA: Who were the cities and kingdoms flourished in this era? What were the major features of these empires?

The Christian States of Nubia: What were the features of the state of Makouria? Who converted them to Christianity and how was this reflected in their culture? What caused their collapse? How did this affect relgion? Identify: Kyriakos, Mamelukes.

The Kingdom of Ethiopia: What fusion took place to revive Ethiopia? What are the striking architectural features from this time period? What renaissance happened under the Solomonids? Identify: Zagwe, Roha, Lalibela, Solomonids, Zara Jacob, Prester John.

A Capital on the Move, a Mountain of Kings: What was the nature of the institution of the traveling court and Mountain of Kings? What were the features of medieval Ethiopia's political system?

The City-States of Zanj: Who moved into the city-states of the Zanj? What factors explain this influx of settlers?

Swahili Culture: What is Swahili and what cultural influences are there in it? Why was East Africa so strategic to trade? What peoples and products were involved? What was life like in these coastal towns according to Portuguese visitors? Identify: Kilwa, Sofala, Mogadishu.

AFRICAN SOCIETY: How did residence, gender and religious patterns effect life for Africans? In what ways was life similar across Inner Africa? How did it differ from West to East?

Urban and Rural Africa: What were the major differences between urban dwellers and rural residents? What was the significance of religion in the lives of each?

Women East and West: How did life differ for African women across the class spectrum? What changes for women accompanied the introduction of Islam? How were African women more free than many of their contemporaries?

Muslim, Christian and Traditional Cultures: What expressions of Muslim and Christian art and architecture can be found in the west and east?

SUMMARY What are the main points of this chapter?

STUDY SKILLS EXERCISES

1. **Making Connections:**
   a. There is a continued theme of monarchs using religion as a way to legitimize their power. How did this develop in West and East Africa both with traditional animistic and major world religions?
   b. These African kingdoms and rulers were contemporary to medieval Europe. As rulers, what common problems did they have and what common tactics did they use?
   c. The name Timbuktu is often used to imply some virtually unknown or remote place. What was it in reality in medieval Africa? Why do you think Westerners were (or are) less likely to know much about it?

2. **Reflection:** Imagine yourself as a traveler such as Ibn Batuta or Al-Bakri. Visit West and then East African cities and write a description of them. To reinforce locations, use the chapter map on p. 312 to explain how you got there and what the overall topography was like using the horizontal belts.

3. **Timeline**
8-11th centuries	Ghana
12th-14th centuries	Mali
1307-1332	Reign of Mansa Musa
6th-14th	Nubia
800	Nubain Makouria's height
12-15th	Ethiopia
12-15th	Zanj

4. **Maps:**
   a. **Age of Expanding Zones of Culture:** (p.233) Be able to locate the two centers of empire in Africa in this period.
   b. **African Empire and Trade Routes:** (p. 312) What types of trade routes were there and what parts of Africa were connected by these routes? What outside areas were these routes connected to? Locate: Ghana Empire, Timbuktu, Niger River, Axum, Mogadishu, Kilwa, Zambezi River, Sofala, Madagascar.

c. Compare the African trade route map above with the Spread of Islam map on p. 261. What connection do you see?

RECITE/REVIEW

Multiple Choice

1. Medieval West African states were geographically oriented to the
   - a. Atlantic coast.
   - b. Indian Ocean.
   - c. south coast of Africa.
   - d. African interior.

2. The most important items in Ghana's trade were
   - a. wine and olive oil.
   - b. Muslin and silk.
   - c. salt and gold.
   - d. furs and skins.

3. The fall of Ghana was due to
   - a. overambition of the kings, attacks of the Almoravids and Saharan expansion.
   - b. civil strife between urban Muslims and outlying traditional animists.
   - c. the interference of Portuguese explorers.
   - d. Muslim military pressure from the Mamelukes and blood schism among the Christians.

4. The name Mali means "Where the _____ Dwells:"
   - a. Mandinke
   - b. King
   - c. Gold
   - d. Salt

5. During this time period in medieval Africa, the West African rulers accepted
   - a. Islam
   - b. Roman Catholic Christianity.
   - c. Buddhism.
   - d. Greek Orthodox Christianity.

6. This famous ruler of West African Mali went on a pilgrimage to Mecca:
   - a. Ibn Batuta
   - b. Zara Jacob
   - c. Lalibela
   - d. Mansa Musa

7. Which one of the following is **NOT** true of medieval Ethiopia?
   - a. Church and state were closely allied.
   - b. It was geographically and religiously isolated.
   - c. It experienced an artistic and literary renaissance.
   - d. Islam formed the basis of its cultural revival.

8. The most significant state of Christian Nubia was
   - a. Zanj.
   - b. Makouria.
   - c. Sofala.
   - d. Mandingo.

9. The Nubian ruling elite were converted to
   - a. Christianity by Greek-speaking Byzantine missionaries.
   - b. Islam by Sufi mystics from Shirazi Persia.
   - c. Shiite Islam by the Mameluke invaders from Egypt.
   - d. Christianity by Roman Catholic bishop from North Africa.

10. Which one of the following has the **LEAST** in common with the others?
    - a. Zagwe
    - b. Roha
    - c. Lalibela
    - d. Sofala

11. This Bantu language was the lingua franca of the eastern coast of Africa:
    - a. Mandinke
    - b. Soninke
    - c. Swahili
    - d. Shirazi

12. If you were a Bantu speaking person with Persian and Arab neighbors, you were probably in this part of medieval Africa:
    a. Zanj
    b. Nubia
    c. Ghana
    d. Mali

13. While kings and the upper class frequently embraced Islam, most Africans practiced
    a. Christianity
    b. Judaism
    c. Traditionalist religions
    d. Hinduism

14. For African women, the spread of Islam might mean less power over
    a. property rights
    b. choosing friends
    c. socializing between the sexes
    d. raising children

15. The Faras frescoes depict
    a. scenes from the Bible
    b. Mansa Musa holding a lump of gold
    c. Portugese traders
    d. Maps of the major trade routes

Short Essay

16. Explain the connection between Mande, Sonike, and Mandinke.
17. What was the cultural zone significance of Mansa Musa's pilgrimage.
18. Describe the Lalibela complex and its cultural zone significance.

Extended Essay

19. Discuss the role of trade in the history of trade in the history of medieval West and East Africa.
20. Describe the culture and achievements of the medieval kingdom of Ethiopia.
21. List the factors that led to the emergence of the West African states and the process of growth that took place. Use specific examples to illustrate your points.

Timeline and Maps

22. Which one of the following was **NOT** contemporary to the other three?
    a. Mali
    b. Ethiopia
    c. Zanj
    d. Ghana

23. As a result of interference and invasion from the Mamelukes, Christian Nubia would have a Muslim dynasty by
    a. 800.
    b. 1000.
    c. 1200.
    d. 1400.

24. One of the major trading cities of medieval West Africa was
    a. Timbuktu
    b. Tuareg.
    c. Kilwa.
    d. Mogadishu.

25. This island off the coast of East Africa was settled by people from Southeast Asia.
    a. Mogadishu.
    b. Mombasa.
    c. Magadascar.
    d. Marrakech.

26. The land of Zanj was located
       a. in West Africa.
       b. north of Nubia.
       c. north of Mali.
       d. in East Africa.

27. East African coastal trade was connected to
       a. Spain and Portugal.
       b. India and China.
       c. Constantinople.
       d. Samarkand.

ANSWERS

Multiple Choice:
1. d, p. 311
2. c, p. 313
3. a, p. 313
4. b, p. 313
5. a, p. 311
6. d, p. 316
7. d, pp. 316-17
8. b, p. 316
9. a, p. 316
10. d, p. 317
11. c, p. 318
12. a, p.318
13. c, p. 319
14. a, p. 319
15. a, p. 319

Short Essay:
16. p. 313
17. p. 316
18. p. 317

Extended Essay:
19. total chapter
20. pp. 316-18
21. pp. 311-16

Timeline and Maps:
22. d, p. 313, 316, 318
23. d, p. 316
24. a, p. 313
25. c, p. 318
26. d, p. 318
27. b, p. 318

24

CONQUERING PEOPLES OF THE AMERICAS: FROM THE TOLTECS TO CHIMU (900-1400)

SURVEY

Chapter Overview: In all the areas of the New World, urban centers continued to develop from Caholia on the Mississippi to Chimu on the coast of Peru. See the chapter outline on p. 321. Read the chapter summary on p. 328.

Chapter Objectives: After reading this chapter and following the study method, you should be able to:

1. Describe the changes in those areas of North America that encouraged the probability of cultures such as the Pueblos and Mississippian.
2. Summarize the features of Pueblo culture.
3. Summarize the features of the Mississippian culture and specifically the Cahokia site.
4. Discuss the accomplishments of the Toltec culture
5. Describe and compare the Peruvian zone sites of Tiahuanaco, Huari and Chimu.
6. Compare the areas of North, Middle and South America at this time.
7. **Making Connections:** Connect the common elements from the Ancient and Classic Age eras (Chapters 9 and 16) to the Middle and South American cultural zones.

QUESTIONS/READ

NORTH AMERIA:THE PUEBLOS AND THE GREAT MOUNDS: What caused the more urban development of the Pueblos and the Great Mounds? What were their features?

Pueblo Culture: What were the features of Pueblo culture? Where was it located? What three crops would encourage transition to village agriculture? Identify: kiva.

The Mississippian Culture: What were the features of Mississippian culture? Where was it located? What were Mississippian sites like? Identify: Cahokia

MIDDLE AMERICA: THE TOLTECS: Who were the Toltecs? What were the major features of their society?

Mexico and Peru: Continuing Centers of American Culture: What were the continuing centers and what was their economic base? What crops supported each areas? Identify: "My Lord, The Corn", quipu.

The Toltecs: A Race of Legendary Heroes: Who were the Toltecs? Where were they located? Why were they called "a race of legendary heroes?" What was the basis of their economy? Identify: Nahuatl, Tula, Chichen Itza, Topilzin.

SOUTH AMERICA: PEOPLES OF THE MOUNTAINS AND THE SHORE: Who were the people of the mountains and those of the shore? What were the features of their societies?

Tiahuanco and Huari: Cities of the Andes: What were these cities? How are they connected? What changes occurred and what are some possible conclusions?

Chimu: People of the Coast: What were the significant features of this society? Identify: Chanchan.

The Power of the Chimu State: Why is the Chimu state believed to have had great central authority?

SUMMARY: What are the main points of the chapter?

STUDY SKILLS EXERCISES

1. **Making Connections:** In relation to Chimu and other large complexes like the ones discussed in the chapter on ancient Egypt, why is great central authority assumed to be necessary? Look at your Overview IV comparison charts to see what trends and varieties of response you can find in the human venture. Compare all four sets of overview charts.

2. **Reflections:** Except for Mississippian, why do you think river systems were not as important as a basis for civilization in the Americas? Why wasn't the Mississippi a site much earlier?

3. **Timeline:**

900-1300	Anasazi
1200s	High point of Cahokia
7-10th centuries	Tiahuanaco and Huari
10-13th centuries	Toltecs
14-15th centuries	Chimu

4. **Maps:**
   a. **Age of Expanding Zones of Culture:** (p. 233) Locate Huari, Tiahuanaco, Anasazi, Cahokia, Toltecs.

RECITE/REVIEW

Multiple Choice

1. A *kiva* was a
   a. underground ceremonial chamber
   b. small ornate doll
   c. granary
   d. small lagoon for collecting water

2. Which one of the following has the **LEAST** to do with the other three?
   a. Pueblo.   c. Anasazi
   b. Kiva   d. Hopewell

3. Mounded complexes like Cahokia are found in
   a. the Mississippi Valley to the U.S. east coat.
   b. Arizona, New Mexico and the northern provinces of Mexico.
   c. Cuba and the islands of the Caribbean.
   d. the Great Plains.

4. The crop that was the basic staff of life in Peru was
   a. maize.   c. wheat.
   b. the potato.   d. beans.

5. The central feature of Toltec culture was the predominance of this class:
   a. merchants   c. warriors
   b. scholars   d. priests

6. Cahokia was to the Mississippian as this was to the Toltecs:
   a. Teotihuacan   c. Quetzelcoatl
   b. Yucatan   d. Tula

7. Important trade goods of the Toltecs were
    a. corn, beans and squash.
    b. cocoa, feathers and cotton.
    c. pottery and the bow and arrow.
    d. gold, salt and bronze.

8. The Toltecs were to Teotihuacan and the Mayas as these were to Mochica:
    a. Chimu
    b. Tiahuanaco
    c. Huari
    d. Curacas

9. Which one of the following was **NOT** a feature of Chimu that assumes well-developed central authority was present?
    a. fortresses
    b. irrigation systems
    c. temples
    d. palaces

Short Essay

10. What does the word Pueblo mean and what is its implication?
11. Why were the Toltecs originally viewed as legendary?
12. How did life in the Andes change under Tiahuanaco-Hurari rule?

Extended Essay

13. Compare the features of the cultural zones of north, Middle and South America.
14. **Making Connections:** Illustrate the connections between the earlier Chavin and Mochica with the cultural zones of Tiahuanco, Huari and Chimu.

Timeline and Maps

15. The Anasazi period was from this century to this century:
    a. 6th-9th
    b. 9th-13th
    c. 10th-14th
    d. 14th-15th

16. The high point of the Cahokia complex was in the
    a. 700s.
    b. 900s.
    c. 1200s.
    d. 1400s.

17. Tiahuanaco and Huari were contemporaries. The time span was
    a. 7-10th centuries.
    b. 11-16th centuries.
    c. 10-13th centuries.
    d. 12-14th centuries.

18. In terms of time, Chimu was
    a. contemporary to Tiahuanaco and Huari.
    b. contemporary to the Toltecs.
    c. at its height in the 14-15th centuries.
    d. close to the Anasazi.

19. Which one of the following was not an Anasazi location?
    a. New Mexico
    b. Arizona
    c. northern provinces of Mexico
    d. Mississippi

20. The modern day location of the Cahokia complex is
    a. St. Louis, Missouri.
    b. New Orleans, Louisiana.
    c. Chicago, Illinois.
    d. Memphis, Tennessee.

21. The Huari, Tiahuanaco and Chimu were centered in the modern-day country of
    a. Guatemala.
    b. Peru.
    c. Brazil.
    d. Mexico.

22. The Toltec culture was centered in
    a. North America
    b. South America.
    c. Mesoameria.
    d. Caribbean.

ANSWERS

Multiple Choice:
1. a, p. 322
2. d, p. 322
3. a, p. 322
4. b, p. 324
5. c, p. 324
6. d, p. 324
7. b, p. 325
8. a, p. 327
9. c, p. 327

Short Essay:
10. p. 322
11. p. 324
12. p. 326

Extended Essay:
13. total chapter
14. chapters 9, 16 and 24

Timeline and Maps:
15. c, p. 322
16. c, p. 323
17. a, p. 326
18. c, p. 327
19. d, p. 322
20. a, p. 322
21. b, p. 326
22. c, p. 324

25

THE HINGE OF HISTORY: FROM PLURALISM TO GLOBALISM

SURVEY

Chapter Overview: By the 1500s, the pluralism of world cultures began to be affected by a greater level of contact with other cultures opening the possibility of a more global culture. At the same time, greater contact spurred a fierce defense of cultural uniqueness. Look at the chapter outline on p. 329. Read the summary on p. 335.

Chapter Objectives: After reading the chapter and following the study method, you should be able to:

1. Explain why the author regards 1500 as a turning point.
2. Discuss the issue of cultural pluralism and the challenge of greater cultural contact.
3. Describe how the West upset the balance of cultures.
4. Discuss the issues involved in the idea of a human community that is global.
5. List the trends that worked against global community.
6. Evaluate various predictions made about a single global culture.
7. **Making Connections:** Use China and India as a model to discuss the possibility that a common global culture does not necessarily mean that there will be political stability or a world government.

QUESTIONS/READ

CULTURAL DIVERSITY: How did cultural diversity develop? What balance was upset by 1500?

1500: An End and a Beginning: Why was 1500 an ending and a beginning point?

Cultural Differences: How did cultural differences develop? How does this vary using an anthropological or sociological viewpoint versus an historical one? Again why is 1500 a significant date?

Centers of Civilization: What were the diverse centers of civilization in 1500? What types of things differentiate one people form another?

A World in Balance: What made it possible for the balance between cultures to emerge and last so long? What types of things brought contacts between the cultures?

TOWARD A GLOBAL COMMUNITY: What changes occurred to make global community a possibility?

Columbus: Upsetting the Balance: Who was Columbus and how did he upset the balance between cultures?

Western Imperialism: What caused the surge of Western imperialism? What made it different from previous imperial ventures? Why was the Western zone of culture more likely to upset the balance? Identify: Cathay, Chipangu, Spice Islands.

Many Histories or One? What two stories will the second text try to tell? What will the various chapters deal with? What key concepts will help to study increasing interdependence?

SUMMARY: What are the main points of this chapter?

STUDY SKILLS EXERCISES

1. **Making Connections:** Look at the maps that accompany the overview divisions of this text. What are the major centers of civilization that have developed by 1500? By 1500 what connections or possibilities of connections had developed between all of those areas?

2. **Timeline:** none in this chapter-review your timeline charts to this 1500 turning point as a way of looking for trends or as a way of review if you have a comprehensive final exam.

3. **Maps:** As a way of review, compare the maps in the overview sections.

RECITE/REVIEW

Multiple Choice

1. Up to 1500, civilizations in Eurasia were characterized by
   a. diversity.   c. complete isolation.
   b. unity.   d. globalism.

2. Which one of the following was **NOT** a way cultural pluralism was maintained?
   a. indifferent to culture.   c. a rough balance of power.
   b. a thinner population.   d. buffer zones of space.

3. Eurasia, Africa and the Americas all had this by 1500:
   a. openness to new cultures   c. regional isolation
   b. major centers of urban culture   d. industrial revolutions

4. When Christopher Columbus set sail from Spain, he assumed he would arrive in
   a. India.   c. the Far East.
   b. North America.   d. Africa.

5. What made Western imperialism different and unprecedented was its
   a. global scale through sea power.
   b. attempts to conquer other people.
   c. land-based power connected to all other cultural zones.
   d. emphasis on political dominance and trade.

6. Up to 1500, human communities basically
   a. stayed isolated from each other.   c. increased in size and complexity.
   b. decreased in size and variety.   d. ignored each other.

7. From 500 to 1500 the effect of common religions, cultures or geographical circumstances was to
   a. expand trade.   c. encourage more wars.
   b. encourage larger cultural zones.   d. encourage homogeneity.

Short Essay

8. What were the centers of civilization in 1500?
9. How did Columbus' voyages change the balance of the world?

Extended Essay

10. Discuss and evaluate 1500 as a turning point in world history.
11. Analyze the trends for and against a global community.
12. **Making Connections:** Using examples from cultures you have studied in this text, evaluate the possibility of a more homogeneous world culture, a world government and/or peace and stability.

Timeline and Maps

13. This date marks the beginning of a point of upsetting the balance in world cultures:
    a. 10,000 B.C.E.
    b. 5000 B.C.E.
    c. C.E. 500
    d. C.E. 1500

ANSWERS

Multiple Choice
1. a, p. 331
2. a, p. 331
3. b, p. 331
4 c, p. 332
5. a, pp. 333-34
6. c, p. 332
7. b, p. 332

Short Essay
8. p. 331
9. p. 332

Extended Essay
10. total chapter
11. total chapter
12. student selected chapters

Timeline and Maps
13. d, p. 332